Understanding Giftedness

This concise, accessible guide explores the different models behind the concept of giftedness, examining the criteria for evaluating and identifying gifted children, in order to provide a deeper understanding of the lives of children and young people with high cognitive potential. It offers practical advice to parents and teachers, highlighting common queries and misconceptions and presenting evidence-based suggestions for management methods.

Key topics covered include the difference between being gifted and talented, how to identify a gifted child, neurological differences between gifted children and their peers, dealing with perfectionism and the best ways to parent and teach a gifted child. Avoiding prescriptive rules, the authors emphasise the importance of knowing and understanding the individual child whilst utilising research around giftedness to promote the best possible outcomes. Illustrated with case studies of student and teacher perspectives, the book offers an inclusive perspective and practical strategies, whereby the development of individual potential is viewed not only as a way to promote the psychological well-being of the individual but also as an opportunity and benefit for society.

Understanding Giftedness is essential reading for parents and caregivers, as well as practitioners in clinical and educational psychology, counselling, mental health, nursing, child welfare, public healthcare and those in education who want to help young people develop their talents and achieve their full potential.

Maria Assunta Zanetti is Associate Professor in the Department of Brain and Behavioral Sciences, University of Pavia, Italy. She is Director of the Italian Laboratory of Research and Intervention for the Development of Talent, Potential and Giftedness at the University of Pavia. She is a member of the committee of the Italian Ministry of Education for the development of gifted and talented guidelines.

Gianluca Gualdi is a psychologist, a psychotherapist and lecturer in developmental psychology at the University of Pavia, Italy. He is involved with LabTalento, in collaboration with the Province of Pavia, running training for high-ability adolescents, training teachers and professionals.

Michael Cascianelli is a School Principal of an international school in Italy where he focuses on the implementation of school-wide enrichment models and the support of gifted and talented students. He is currently developing his research at the Faculty of Education of the University of Cambridge, UK.

Understanding Atypical Development
Series editor: Alessandro Antonietti,
Università Cattolica del Sacro Cuore, Italy

This volume is one of a rapidly developing series in *Understanding Atypical Development*, published by Routledge. This book series is a set of basic, concise guides on various developmental disorders or issues of atypical development. The books are aimed at parents, but also professionals in health, education, social care and related fields, and are focused on providing insights into the aspects of the condition that can be troubling to children, and what can be done about it. Each volume is grounded in scientific theory but with an accessible writing style, making them ideal for a wide variety of audiences.

Each volume in the series is published in hardback, paperback and eBook formats. More information about the series is available on the official website at: www.routledge.com/Understanding-Atypical-Development/book-seriesUATYPDEV, including details of all the titles published to date.

Published Titles

Understanding Tourette Syndrome
Carlotta Zanaboni Dina and Mauro Porta

Understanding Rett Syndrome
Rosa Angela Fabio, Tindara Caprì and Gabriella Martino

Understanding Conduct Disorder and Oppositional-Defiant Disorder
Laura Vanzin and Valentina Mauri

Understanding Giftedness
Maria Assunta Zanetti, Gianluca Gualdi and Michael Cascianelli

Understanding Giftedness

A Guide for Parents and Educators

Edited by Maria Assunta Zanetti, Gianluca Gualdi and Michael Cascianelli

LONDON AND NEW YORK

First published 2020
by Routledge
2 Park Square, Milton Park, Abingdon, Oxon OX14 4RN

and by Routledge
52 Vanderbilt Avenue, New York, NY 10017

Routledge is an imprint of the Taylor & Francis Group, an informa business

© 2020 Maria Assunta Zanetti, Gianluca Gualdi and Michael Cascianelli

The right of Maria Assunta Zanetti, Gianluca Gualdi and Michael Cascianelli to be identified as authors of this work has been asserted by them in accordance with sections 77 and 78 of the Copyright, Designs and Patents Act 1988.

All rights reserved. No part of this book may be reprinted or reproduced or utilised in any form or by any electronic, mechanical, or other means, now known or hereafter invented, including photocopying and recording, or in any information storage or retrieval system, without permission in writing from the publishers.

Trademark notice: Product or corporate names may be trademarks or registered trademarks, and are used only for identification and explanation without intent to infringe.

British Library Cataloguing-in-Publication Data
A catalogue record for this book is available from the British Library

Library of Congress Cataloging-in-Publication Data
A catalog record has been requested for this book

ISBN: 978-1-138-32116-8 (hbk)
ISBN: 978-1-138-32117-5 (pbk)
ISBN: 978-0-429-45281-9 (ebk)

Typeset in Sabon
by Swales & Willis, Exeter, Devon, UK

Contents

About the editors ix

Preface xi

PART I
Understanding giftedness 1

1 An in-depth look at giftedness 3
MARIA ASSUNTA ZANETTI

2 The gifted adolescent world 43
MARIA ASSUNTA ZANETTI AND GIANLUCA GUALDI

3 Learning for gifted students is not so easy 61
MARIA ASSUNTA ZANETTI

4 Educating gifted and talented students in everyday
school practice 72
MICHAEL CASCIANELLI

5 Being a parent of gifted children and adolescents:
personal strategies to support growth 91
GIANLUCA GUALDI

PART II
Supporting gifted students in school 103

6 Watching the plants grow: understanding
giftedness in science 105
KEITH S. TABER

viii Contents

7 Teachers' conceptions of giftedness and gifted
education: an international perspective   128
DANIEL HERNÁNDEZ-TORRANO

8 Implementing Schoolwide Enrichment Model for
talent development: perspectives from students and
teachers in Italy   148
MICHAEL CASCIANELLI

Index   169

About the editors

Maria Assunta Zanetti, PhD is Associate Professor at the University of Pavia, Dept. of Brain and Behavioral Sciences. She is currently teaching Psychology of Language Development and Educational Psychology. She collaborates with the Italian Ministry of Education (MIUR) and other local institutions to promote mental health and is leading several national and international projects to support well-being in schools. Her main research interests include socio-emotional development, youth risk behaviours, language development, bullying and cyberbullying, vocational guidance, decision-making processes, early achievement, and gifted children development. She participated in several research projects in the Developmental and Educational Psychology areas. Since 2001 she has been a counsellor for guidance in the pre-university area. Presently, she is President of the Guidance and Vocational Centre of the University of Pavia (COR – Centro di Orientamento) and Director of the Italian Laboratory of Research and Intervention for the Development of Talent, Potential and Giftedness at the University of Pavia. Since 2015 she has been vice-president the Centre for Research on Gender at the University of Pavia and a member of the Strategic Project Migrat-IN-G, University of Pavia. She has published several papers, book chapters and handbooks, mainly focusing on socio-emotional development and resilience, behavioural problems, bullying and cyberbullying, early achievement and giftedness, and vocational guidance. She is a member of the following organisations:

- AIP – Associazione Italiana Psicologia
- SIO – Società Italiana di Orientamento (Italian Society for Vocational Guidance)

- AERA – American Educational Research Association
- ENSEC – European Network for Social and Emotional Competence
- CKBG – Collaborative Knowledge Building Group

Michael Cascianelli is a Master's graduate and PhD researcher from the University of Cambridge. He has worked in the field of education, teaching and researching in different contexts such as the United Kingdom, The Netherlands, Italy, China and Thailand. He is currently a School Principal in an international school in Italy where he also focuses on the implementation of Schoolwide Enrichment Models and the support of gifted and talented students. His main research interests include giftedness, intelligence and talent development as well as leadership and emotional intelligence.

Gianluca Gualdi is a psychologist and psychotherapist (systemic-relational and EMDR). He works in mother–child and minor educational communities as a psychologist and coordinator. He has carried out projects in schools (socio-emotional learning, school orientation and promotion of skills) and teacher training (school guidance and resilience) and currently works externally with LabTalento for group activities for high-ability adolescents, training teachers and professionals. He leads the course "Emotional and relational aspects of development" at the University of Pavia and teaches on the Master's course "Immigration, gender, family models and integration strategies".

Preface

The book is intended as a guide to understanding the topic of high cognitive potential. About 5% of the population has an IQ greater than 130 and this is associated with behavioural characteristics and specific educational needs. The topic is explored by starting from a theoretical framework, after which the book analyses the evaluation and identification criteria of high cognitive potential and suggested management methods, both in the family and the school context. Finally, case studies analysing multiple perspectives of students' and teachers' perspectives are provided together with implementation strategies to use in the school context. The authors of the book have adopted an inclusive perspective which sees the development of individual potential not only as a way to promote the psychological well-being of the individual but also as an opportunity and resource for all. The book, therefore, offers an initial response to all children, parents and teachers and school administrators who are living with or managing this condition to avoid dispersing human potential and capital.

The aim of this book is to help support gifted children, covering topics such as understanding a child's giftedness, dealing with perfectionism in gifted children, and helping them to develop their talents and achieve their full potential.

Part I

Understanding giftedness

Chapter 1

An in-depth look at giftedness

Maria Assunta Zanetti

Definition of giftedness and talent

Ask 100 people what is meant by giftedness and you will likely get 100 different definitions, even if some common elements emerge from most of the descriptions. These might include describing a person's aptitude in a specific subject area or a talent in the visual or performing arts or in sports. Also mentioned might be creativity, inventiveness, or just plain "intelligent in everything". That becomes a major problem when deciding who is gifted.

Most of the literature investigated refers to gifted learners as pupils who display higher abilities, more creativity, and more motivation to learn than other pupils in similar age groups. Giftedness is usually understood in relation to intelligence (see European Commission, 2006). However, giftedness is not an easy term to define and it also varies a great deal depending on the context in which it is being used. Drawing on George (1992 in White, Fletcher-Campbell, & Ridley, 2003), for example, there are over 200 definitions of "giftedness".

The adopted term, by its origin, gives clues to understanding the concept of ability which puts great emphasis on genetic hereditability and therefore some characteristics defined as talent, i.e., "any capacity that enables an individual to display exceptionally high performance in a domain that requires special skills and training" (Simonton, 1999). Talent was the name given and whoever possessed talents was talented, suggesting something that can be acquired. Ability indicates "power to learn and act"; that is, to capture elements within the everyday living environment, and to abstract, organize, and incorporate this material into the internal perceptual field and to express it in proper ways of behaving.

Natural ability has its origins in genetic hereditability, which is configured by the combination of chromosomes in strings of genes, into a unique, individual, probably unrepeatable organization of its own. The old debate around "heredity versus environment" gives space to the authority of scientific knowledge (Plomin, 1998). The term "innate", as well as the term "natural", means "present at birth" without being necessarily hereditary. Strictly speaking, the term "innate" is a metaphorical reference, which means "being like this since birth" (Gagné & Guenther, 2010).

Another kind of ability influencing human life is acquired ability, reached through learned behavior (Angoff, 1988), which is developed by the influence of intentional environmental forces. The amount of possible acquired ability for any individual is conditioned by the level of natural ability predicted as potential in genetic hereditability.

In research literature and psychology textbooks there is a wide range of different terms used to describe young people displaying all forms of giftedness. These terms may cover very different concepts depending on their origin, their historical context, and what is meant by intelligence and denoted talent. Furthermore, the terminology adopted appears to be related to the educational policies developed for the benefit of these young people (Eurydice Report, 2006, p. 7).

This statement demonstrates the importance of defining what giftedness is in order to understand how different countries respond to such a phenomenon in terms of policy and practice. However, the definition of "gifted and talented" learners is most commonly used in conceptualizing the term "gifted", which usually indicates pupils with high academic achievements and in conceptualizing the term "talented", which instead refers to pupils with high performance in sports and arts (White, Fletcher-Campbell, & Ridley, 2003).

The question concerning the meaning of giftedness shows the importance of understanding giftedness as a fluid concept which should not only be considered in terms of "genetic or innate abilities", but as a multi-faceted notion (Borland, 2005; Smith, 2006; Sternberg & Davidson, 2005). Giftedness manifests itself in different forms which require a variety of contexts and learning opportunities capable of grasping the totality of pupils' abilities. So, for example, Sternberg and Davidson (2005) discuss the fact that giftedness is something created by society rather than something we discover, and therefore its conceptualization can change over time and place. For this reason, it is very important to understand how the notion of giftedness is conceptualized in different countries and how such a conceptualization may impact upon policies and practice. The descriptions of giftedness furthermore vary from one culture to another. Gifted abilities are also more likely to emerge when the individual's talents coincide with what is valued by the culture. Chess prodigies, for example, appear in cultures where such talent is valued and nurtured. Giftedness is what society perceives to be higher or lower on some culturally embedded scale.

Even researchers in gifted education have a difficult time agreeing on what giftedness means, but they agree on one thing: giftedness derives from a well above average level of intelligence in one or more observable behaviors. So, before we can understand what makes a person gifted, we have to take a closer look at what modern research has discovered about intelligence.

For many years in gifted education, the terms "gifted" and "talented" were often used interchangeably and attempts to differentiate them were only moderately successful. Indeed, some researchers saw no real difference between the two. In the 1980s, Gagné (1985) proposed a comprehensive model that made a distinction between the components of giftedness and the nature of talent.

Gagné (2003) differentiates between giftedness and talent, proposing that giftedness represents innate abilities in multiple domains, while talent is a skill in a single domain that has been systematically developed. The innate abilities fall into four aptitude domains: *intellectual, creative, socioaffective,* and *sensorimotor*. These aptitudes have a genetic basis and can be readily observed in the tasks that children perform in school. A Differentiated Model of Giftedness and Talent (DMGT) described the process of talent development as the transformation of above-average natural abilities, spontaneously possessed by an individual (called gift), into systematically developed expert performance. Such transformation is possible thanks to the operation of some catalysts connected to: interpersonal aspects (e.g.,

6 Maria Assunta Zanetti

motivation, interests, habits), environmental variables (e.g., socio-demographic factors or the influence of parents, teachers, or peers), specific structures and programs of talent development, or genetic predisposition (Gagné, 1985).

Gagné described the model in its original version of 1985, but it has been updated several times (Gagné, 2004, 2009) until its last version in 2013. In 2009, Gagné also updated his definition of the talent development process to:

> the systematic pursuit by talentees, over a significant and continuous period of time, of a structured program of activities leading to a specific excellence goal [where talentee indicates] anyone participating in a systematic talent development program, whatever the field.
>
> (Gagné, 2009)

Talents in this model emerge from a developmental process that transforms aptitudes into the skills that are characteristic of a particular field of human activity or performance. The model indicates that abilities and aptitudes are the raw constituents of talent.

In other words, talent implies the presence of well above-average natural abilities. One cannot be talented without having gifts. However, according to Gagné (2003), the opposite is also true. Some students with well above-average natural abilities do not translate these gifts into talents, as evidenced by academic underachievement in intellectually gifted students.

In summary, the terms "giftedness" and "talent" are identified as:

Giftedness indicates a "competence which is distinctly above average in one or more domains of ability" (Gagné, 1985), a definition that was recently updated to: "the possession and use of untrained and spontaneously expressed outstanding natural abilities or aptitudes (called gifts), in at least one ability domain, to a degree that places an individual at least among the top 10% of age peers" (Gagné, 2013).

Talent, on the other hand, defines a "performance which is distinctly above average in one or more fields of human performance" (Gagné, 1985), a definition recently updated to: "the outstanding mastery of systematically developed competencies (knowledge and skills) in at least one field of human activity to a degree that places an individual at least among the top 10% of 'learning peers'" (Gagné, 2013).

In the 2013 updated version of DMGT Gagné added two important changes (Gagné, 2013):

The first concerned the biological underpinnings of DMGT, or the genotypic foundations of gifts, which influence both the physiological endo-phenotype – a set of non-externally visible but measurable physical characteristics, like aerobic capacity – and the anatomical exo-phenotype – the external and visible set of characteristics which influence abilities and behaviors (e.g., resistance or agility). Gagné underlined that there is no direct connection between the biological underpinnings of giftedness and the expression of giftedness itself, but rather it is mediated by the action of catalysts. Introducing the biological underpinnings of giftedness, Gagné described the Developmental Model of Natural Abilities (known as DMNA), which explains how giftedness results from the process of transformation of biological underpinnings. Subsequently Gagné introduced the Expanded Model of Talent Development – EMTD, which integrates the DMGT with DMNA, to obtain a complex model of talent development. It begins with the emergence of giftedness from its biological underpinnings and finishes with the expression and development of a specific talent, through the action of a set of catalysts. DMNA and DMGT are not clearly divided and do not occur in the same way for everybody because a lot depends on the action of catalysts and the specific area of talent (e.g., time of maturation in sport can be very different than in science, literature, or medicine). Thus, Gagné concludes that:

Talent development results from a complex series of interactions between the four groups of causal components; it becomes a choreography unique to each individual.

(Gagné, 2013)

Therefore, it is wrong and misleading to consider the concepts of giftedness and talent as synonyms. They must be clearly differentiated between gifts (natural abilities) and talents (systematically developed from gifts).

These definitions allow us to conceive talent development as the progressive transformation of outstanding natural abilities (gifts) into outstanding knowledge and skills (talents) in a specific occupational field. Outstanding natural abilities (gifts) from one or more domains may be viewed as raw materials in the talent development process. The talent development process can be supported or hindered by intrapersonal and/or environmental catalysts. These are factors, in addition to cognitive and intellectual ability, that help us better understand and even predict the unfolding and development of talent at the highest levels of expertise and even eminence.

It is important then to not only recognize the presence of high ability or talent but also to observe its development.

The existence of talent is, in itself, something of a mystery: originated in the intimacy of the genes' combination happening a few hours after the conception of a new being, a talent lies there as a seed that needs appropriate conditions to develop and grow. At that stage it would be generically called a "gift", a "natural ability", or an "innate predisposition". Later on, when it is confirmed in the environment, with an acknowledged high-level behavior, we essentially recognize it as "acquired", or absorbed from the surrounding environment.

Ability and talent exist and this is an undisputed fact. They should not be thought of as a personal trait, or a block of features, but as a natural phenomenon captured in different dimensions and manifestations, by a wide diversity of expressions. Talent as such is found in all social groups, all races and people, in all geographies and throughout all history. A considerable body of research aligns studies indicating a strong association between human ability and genetic configuration, reaching as high as 70%, without considering the set of elements, influences, and active environmental interaction networks acting in different life stages.

Giftedness manifests itself as a cluster of traits, not as a typical pattern of behavior and development. High-ability young children vary in the range of talents they exhibit and in their emotional, social, and physical development. They may demonstrate outstanding development in one or in many areas. Young children's development is dynamic and individual. One child may exhibit outstanding reasoning ability and poor manipulative skills, another child may have highly developed verbal skills but little ability to write or draw accurately, and yet another child may hide their abilities in order to "fit in" with their peers.

Are there a lot of myths about gifted children?

Gifted children are smart, so they can get by on their own. When students are not presented with learning experiences that are appropriate for their abilities, they lose motivation and sometimes even interest in learning and in school. Brain research suggests that the brain will not maintain its level of development if students are not challenged.

Gifted students excel in all school subjects

There are students who are high achievers in all areas while many others have subject-specific strengths. Gifted students may struggle in some subjects or activities, while they soar in others. Some gifted students even have learning disabilities.

Gifted students are a heterogeneous group

Just like any other group, gifted students have different interests, areas of strength, ability levels, and temperaments. There is not a definitive list of gifted characteristics, nor will all students' needs be met with the same strategies. Providing differentiated instruction is a necessity, even in advanced classes.

All children are gifted

This is a well-intentioned belief and it is true that all children can learn and all children have areas of strength. Nevertheless, it is a fact that some students learn more quickly and are capable of a higher level of work than their age peers. Gifted students need different contents and instructions in order to meet their needs.

The concept

The central nervous system of an individual contains the roots of their abilities in terms of innate aptitude, potential, and predispositions of their genetic hereditability. By examining studies on brain organization (Clark, 1992) it is possible to abstract areas of brain functions which are located to specific areas of human ability and talent.

The concept of giftedness in the 20th century has become a subject of great investigation. Early studies demonstrated that gifted students are not socially or emotionally bereft and are often successful throughout their lives (e.g., Terman, 1925).

Initially the concept of giftedness has relied on testing for high IQ levels. The broad field that giftedness has become had at its roots in a narrow definition and middle- to upper-class aspirations.

The American historic definition of giftedness, contained in the Marland Report given by the NAGC (National Association for Gifted Children), states that:

> Gifted individuals are those who demonstrate outstanding levels of aptitude (defined as an exceptional ability to reason and learn) or competence (documented performance or achievement in top 10% or rarer) in one or more domains. Domains include any structured area of activity with its own symbol system (e.g., mathematics, music, language) and/or set of sensorimotor skills (e.g., painting, dance, sports).
>
> (2010)

In 1978 Renzulli proposed a definition which received worldwide recognition and was used extensively throughout the 1980s.

Giftedness consists of an interaction among three basic clusters of human traits:

- above-average general abilities
- high levels of task commitment
- high levels of creativity

VanTassel-Baska (1998) has expanded the conceptions of giftedness. She explained how the notion of genius has been extended to embrace creativity (Guilford, 1950; Torrance, 1967), talent development (Feldhusen, 1995; Renzulli, 1994; VanTassel-Baska, 1998), componential intelligence (Sternberg, 1986, 1991), and multiple intelligences (Gardner, 1993; Gardnerd, 1983). Another expansion of the concept of giftedness is seen in Gagné's (1985, 1995, 2000) theory of giftedness and talent where he proposes a set of aptitudes or gifts which the child develops into talents through interaction with a range of internal and external catalysts. However, the gifted field has debated these issues for over 30 years (Gallagher, 2008).

Some authors align with traditional psychometric conceptions of giftedness, emphasizing high intellectual ability. A few authors emphasize the multidimensionality of the construct, highlighting the importance of cultural dimension.

Recently, Pfeiffer (2013a) proposed a tripartite model of giftedness, which is essentially a synthesis of traditional psychometric, developmental, transformational, and ecological models.

The tripartite model provides three different but compatible ways to view giftedness and three compatible but alternative ways to assess giftedness: giftedness viewed as high intelligence, giftedness viewed as outstanding accomplishments, and giftedness viewed as high potential to excel.

The tripartite model offers options for identifying gifted students based on viewing the construct: through the lens of high intelligence, through the lens of outstanding accomplishments, or through the lens of potential to excel (Pfeiffer, 2015). The tripartite model does not stipulate specific thresholds or cutoff scores for inclusion or exclusion into any one of the three alternative types of giftedness; the model leaves this decision to those who are responsible for overseeing gifted education programs (Pfeiffer, 2013b), preferably at the local level (Lohman, 2009). A student can be mildly gifted, moderately gifted, highly gifted, or exceptionally gifted within any one of the three types of giftedness in the tripartite model. Of course, far fewer students will be highly or exceptionally gifted than mildly or moderately gifted. Also, assessment becomes more broadly defined within this model. For example, evidence of outstanding accomplishments can include authentic assessment of creative products or creative performances (Kaufman & Plucker, 2011; Kaufman, Plucker, & Baer, 2008).

Our findings suggest that while some definitions have expanded beyond the traditional cognitive perspective, there is not yet a consensus on how giftedness is defined even among a homogeneous group of test authors.

We can ultimately consider giftedness as a complex constellation of personal and behavioral characteristics which are viewed and expressed in multiple and different ways (Renati & Zanetti, 2012; Zanetti, 2014a).

The other side of the moon

Gifted children have the same basic needs as other children and progress through the same developmental stages as other children (though often at a younger age) and can be confronted with the same problems (such as family poverty, substance abuse, or alcoholism). Nevertheless, research indicates that there are needs and problems that appear more often among gifted children (Webb & Kleine, 1993). In addition, there are three important factors that interact to influence a gifted child's well-being: type of giftedness, educational fit, and personal characteristics (Neihart, 1999).

Research suggests that none of the conclusions can be drawn for gifted children. A great deal of research has been conducted over the past fifty years on the impact of giftedness on psychological well-being. There is research to support two apparently conflicting views on the effects of giftedness: giftedness increases resiliency and it increases vulnerability in gifted children.

Intellectually or academically gifted children who are achieving and participate in special educational programs for gifted students are at least as well adjusted as and perhaps better adjusted than their non-gifted peers. These children do not seem to be more at risk for social or emotional problems than others. It is clear from the research that giftedness does influence psychological outcomes for people, but whether those outcomes are positive or negative seems to depend on several factors that interact synergistically. These factors are the type and degree of giftedness, the educational fit or lack thereof, and one's personal characteristics.

In a comprehensive review of the literature, Nancy Robinson and Kate Noble report:

> Perusal of a large group of studies of preadolescent children revealed [that] ... as a group, gifted children were seen as more trustworthy, honest, socially competent, assured and comfortable with self, courteous, cooperative, stable, and humorous, while they were also seen as showing diminished tendencies to boast, to engage in delinquent activity, to aggress or withdraw, to be domineering, and so on.
>
> (Robinson & Noble, 1991, p. 62)

An in-depth look at giftedness 13

However, other research suggests that gifted children are vulnerable to social and emotional difficulties. Gifted students' social adjustment may vary depending on the level of giftedness. The criticality can be traced to four factors:

- Asynchrony
- Difficulty in finding peers
- Lack of challenge
- Personal characteristics

Gifted children's needs arise because of the interaction with the environmental setting which includes family, school, and culture, and those that arise internally because of the personality of the gifted child. Therefore their characteristics represent strengths on the one hand, but can also be associated with potential problems.

These characteristics are not always a problem in themselves, but a combination can result in the following behavioral problems.

Gifted children often have substantial variations in abilities within themselves and develop unevenly across various skill areas. This uneven pattern of behavior is called "asynchronous development" (Webb, Gore, Amend, & DeVries, 2007, p. 7).

Asynchrony shows a delay between advanced cognitive abilities compared to chronological age and motor development aligned with age, especially in gifted preschool children (Webb & Kleine, 1993). All of the activities these children wish to carry out are obstructed by their motor skills, resulting in intense frustration and emotional outbursts.

As preschoolers and in primary grades, gifted children (particularly highly gifted) attempt to organize people and things. Their search for consistency emphasizes "rules," which they attempt to apply to others. They invent complex games and try to organize their playmates, often inducing resentment in their peers. Moreover, the ability to see possibilities and alternatives may imply that youngsters see idealistic images of what they might be, and simultaneously berate themselves because they see how they are falling short of an ideal (Aderholt-Elliott, 1989; Powell & Haden, 1984). Another element that can be critical is perfectionism: gifted children can have unrealistically high expectations of themselves and this can hinder both academic and professional achievements. The way gifted youngsters see possibilities is the same way they see potential problems in undertaking activities. They will probably avoid potential problems, resulting in under-achievement (Whitmore, 1980).

Gifted children often have several advanced capabilities and may be involved in diverse activities to an almost frantic degree. Though this is seldom a problem for the child, it may create problems for the family, as well as quandaries when decisions must be about career choice (Kerr, 1985, 1991).

However, some critical issues that gifted students live are also due to the lack of knowledge and therefore of understanding of their characteristics by the scholastic and social contexts.

It is therefore important that teachers and educators are pre-pared to offer these children adequate recognition and support. In addition, their behaviors are often not in line with adult expectations, as their creativity and advanced level of reasoning over peers create discomfort or make them at risk of exclusion and depression.

Gifted students' social adjustment may vary depending on the level of giftedness. For instance, early research by Hollingworth (1926, 1942) found that children with intellectual ability scores between 125 and 155 were within the "optimal" range for confidence and friendship. However, Hollingworth noted that children with ability scores above 160 were unlikely to find peers who were similar in interests and abilities and therefore felt more socially isolated. Hollingworth indicated that this was especially true for younger children – five to nine years of age.

The gap created between cognitive aspects and socio-emotional aspects has been described as a discrepancy by some (Terrassier) and called dissincronia by others (Dabrowski and Piechowski).

The term dyssynchrony is used to indicate the psychological and social consequences of irregular development in gifted chil-dren (Terrassier, 2004). It indicates the suffering that children experience with respect to the level difference in the development of intellectual, affective, and motor skills. This is reflected in their daily lives with the risk of psychological problems. Terras-sier has two aspects (1985): internal and social dyssynchrony.

Asynchrony and dyssynchrony refer to similar phenomena. The term dyssynchrony refers to something difficult and negative, concerning the field of pathology. The term asynchrony instead highlights the cognitive and emotional potential of children, which is highlighted when combining high intelligence with a strong sensitivity. Furthermore, the second term incorporates Dabrowski's notion of intensity.

For gifted students, one of the possible risk factors at a psychological level is overexcitability, which is a form of response that the child performs in a situation of difficulty/crisis, whereby they tend to use their own intellectual potential to regulate their emotionality and physical activation (Dąbrowski & Piechowski, 1977). This concept derives from Dabrowski's theory on the development of potential (1964) in which five different types of overexcitabilities are defined. For Dabrowski there are five ways of responding to stimuli that testify to a surplus of nervous energy:

- *psychomotor overexcitability*, which presupposes an accelerated speech (rapid speech and nail-biting), intense athletic activity, inability to stand still, immediate reaction to impulses, and workaholic and delinquent behavior;
- *sensorial overexcitability*, which is the need for physical contact – to receive caresses or to be the center of attention;
- *imaginative overexcitability*, which is related to the increase in mental associations of images and impressions, manifested through dreams, nightmares, or alternation of fiction and reality (day-dreaming, fantasy, magical and metaphorical thought, and poetic or dramatic interpretations of events);
- *intellectual overexcitability*, with which we mean the tendency to ask questions and to want to know incessantly;
- *emotional overexcitability*, which includes emotional inhibition (shyness or shame) and concern for death, anxiety, fear, depressive experiences, feelings of loneliness, and concern for others.

According to Piechowski (1999), overexcitability can enrich, nurture, and reinforce the abilities of high-potential children, but also intensify personal introspection related to perfectionism and the tendency to set unrealistic/unachievable goals. A continuous and deep introspection allows a self-knowledge, but with the tendency to be more sensitive to any type of frustration. This aspect emerges in particular when one is in relationship with others, which is not always predictable; the simplest defense strategy is therefore the closure of relationships as avoidance of difficulty. This aspect can lead to social closures, with exclusion or social withdrawal, in particular toward the peer group (Tieso, 2007).

Asynchrony is understood as "out-of-sync" (Silverman, 2002) and in gifted students it is the tendency to have superior intellectual abilities to chronological age, with physical abilities in the norm of age. This difference in balance leads the child to experience emotional and social stress. This situation is riskier for twice-exceptional children.

These behaviors are referred to as "asynchronous development in which advanced cognitive abilities and increased intensity combine to create inner experiences and awareness about one's own diversity from the norm". This awareness does not always exist and in these cases children risk developing an emotional-behavioral disorder.

In the realm of socio-emotional development gifted students have been found to have high self-concepts and to be highly motivated, well adjusted, socially mature, and independent (Neihart et al., 2002).

Practical suggestions

Is my son gifted? If so, what can I do?

Giovanni is 6 years old. He is a very lively and curious boy and has always been precocious in tackling the stages of development; he learned to read at the age of 3 and started talking very fluently with a wide range of vocabulary. He is very interested in atoms, in the mechanism of things, and he is always looking for new stimuli.

Can he be considered as a gifted child?

At school and in everyday life there are those who excel at performing tasks and activities. We have all had some experience with people who learn with greater naturalness compared to us.

Do they have any superpowers? Do they use special tricks?
Absolutely not.
What we must refer to is intelligence, but what is intelligence and how do we define it?
The research has well defined what intelligence is and how it can be sustained through adequate stimuli. It is now clear that what we define as IQ is considered to be something innate, which differs from person to person and that follows its biological maturation,

but which is also sensibly linked to the environment and to the contexts in which the person is immersed and develops in.

Intelligence is indeed a personal and unique characteristic, but it must be cultivated, otherwise there is a risk of it being dispersed. Parents of gifted children should always keep in mind that their children are above all children, with emotional needs and common issues to their peers. They should not be forced to perform, but parents should support their children's cognitive needs in relation to a psycho-emotional balance. It is important for parents not to be frightened by precociousness and not to cease to exercise their supporting role, and their transmission of love, approval, and respect for rules.

What can you do if you have a high-achievement child? Would it be better to leave them free to explore or push them to achieve their goals?

Ensure that your child has everything they need to develop their skills. Help them recognize their interests and cultivate them and take them forward thoroughly. Avoid dispersing talent and remember that multi-potentiality becomes a risk factor.

Allow your child to have some unstructured time each day just to think, play, and daydream. It is important for creativity and having some downtime could prevent your child from becoming stressed.

You don't have to spend a fortune or always satisfy their requests. You can also support their learning at home to expand their knowledge of subjects taught in school.

What support do gifted children need?

The same as any other child. Gifted children tend to be very hard on themselves, so you may need to provide and offer your support if they are trying very difficult things. Allow them to fail and manage failures. If they succeed all the time, it could lead to too much pressure on themselves. Failure can be difficult, but it helps them learn and develop their skills. Gifted children can be misunderstood as they often learn differently, interact differently, and don't quite conform to "normal behavior".

Discuss your child's qualities and characteristics with family members, friends, other parents, teachers, and club leaders so that

18 Maria Assunta Zanetti

they can try to understand your child and what is "normal" for them. It should help your child feel more accepted and at ease.

Profiles of the gifted and talented

Gifted children are usually discussed as an undifferentiated group. Instead, although they may have common characteristics for some aspects, there are different types of gifted individuals. However, there is no clear division of the types, and a combination is always possible. When they are differentiated, it tends to be on the basis of differences in intellectual abilities, talents, or interests rather than from a total or "gestalt" point of view in terms of behavior, feelings, and needs.

Personality is the result of life experiences and genetic makeup. Not all gifted children are affected by their special abilities in the same way. Gifted children interact with and are influenced by their families, their education, their relationships, and their personal development. Experience with gifted children in a variety of settings has served to increase awareness that the gifted cannot be seen as one group (Strang, 1965).

Giftedness should not be defined by separate categories; every aspect of personality and development influences and interacts with every other aspect. Giftedness should be examined as a construct that impacts on personality.

Specifically, Betts and Neihart (1988) find six different types of giftedness:

- Type 1: The successful
- Type 2: The challenging
- Type 3: The underground
- Type 4: The dropouts
- Type 5: The double labeled
- Type 6: The autonomous learner

Type 1

The successful are the most easily identifiable in schools (about 90% of the identified gifted students). They are the students who have learnt the system and are well adjusted to society with a generally high self-concept. They are obedient, display appropriate behavior,

An in-depth look at giftedness   19

and are high achievers, and therefore are loved by parents and teachers. After discovering what "sells" at home and at school, they begin to display appropriate behavior. They learn well and are able to score high on achievement tests and tests of intelligence.

However, they can also get bored at school and learn the system fast enough so as to use the minimum effort to get by. They are also dependent on the system, thus less creative and imaginative, and lack autonomy. They are dependent upon parents and teachers. They fail to learn needed skills and attitudes for autonomy, but they do achieve.

Gifted young adults who may underachieve in college and later adulthood come from this group. They do not possess the skills, concepts, and attitudes necessary for life-long learning. They are well adjusted to society but are not well prepared for the ever-changing challenges of life.

Strategies for parents

Give them more independence and freedom. Provide them with chances to take risks.

Strategies for teachers

Allow them to accelerate or have an enriched curriculum. Make sure they are able to interact with like-minded peers and allow them time to explore personal interests.

Type 2

The challenging are the divergently gifted, who possess high levels of creativity (many school systems fail to identify Type 2 gifted children). They do not conform to the system and often have conflicts with teachers and parents. They get frustrated, as the school system does not recognize their abilities. They may be seen as disruptive in the classroom and often possess negative self-concepts, even though they are quite creative. This is the group of gifted students who are at risk of dropping out of schools for unhealthy activities, like getting involved in drugs or exhibiting delinquent behavior. They may appear to be obstinate, tactless, or sarcastic and challenge the teacher in front of the class.

Strategies for parents

Be your child's advocate at school. Accept them and try to understand them as best you can. Let them explore their interests.

Strategies for teachers

Place students with a teacher that is able to understand and meet their needs. Have clear, direct communication with the student. Help the student improve social and behavior skills.

Type 3

The underground are gifted students who deny their talents or hide their potential in order to feel more included with a non-gifted peer group. They are generally females (of middle school, males in high school), who are frequently insecure and anxious as their belonging needs rise dramatically at that stage (Kerr, 1985).

Their needs may be different from the expectations of parents and teachers, with the feeling of not being acceptable for what they are.

Parents and teachers often press to promote the skills and potential of these students. At the same time these pressures are experienced by the student as a non-recognition of self, with consequent closure, anxiety, and refusal to show themselves as they are.

Strategies for parents

Accept the child for who they are and provide the necessary time to understand each other and space for comparison with children of their age and/or with the same characteristics.

Strategies for teachers

Let students take breaks from gifted classes if they want to. Believing in the potential of the student, without rejecting it, promotes short- to medium-term needs.

Type 4

The dropouts are the angry and frustrated students whose needs have not been recognized for many years and they feel rejected in the system. They express themselves by being depressed or withdrawn and responding defensively. They are identified very late; therefore, they are bitter and resentful because of feelings of neglect and have very low self-esteem. For these students, counseling is highly recommended. Frequently, Type 4s have interests that lie outside the realm of the regular school curriculum and they fail to receive support and affirmation for their talent and interest in these unusual areas. School seems irrelevant and perhaps hostile to them.

Strategies for parents

Activate a psychological and/or psychotherapeutic support for the student and for the parents. A psychodiagnostic evaluation is important for identifying risk factors and resources (particularly in adolescence).

Strategies for teachers

Create learning experiences outside the classroom for the student. Allow them the ability to study subjects in-depth. Traditional programming is no longer appropriate.

Type 5

The double labeled are gifted students who are physically or emotionally handicapped in some way, or have a learning disability. They show signs of stress, frustration, rejection, helplessness, or isolation. They are also often impatient and critical with low self-esteem. These students are easily ignored as they are seen as average. School systems seem to focus more on their weaknesses, and therefore fail to nurture their strengths (Daniels, 1983; Fox, Brody, & Tobin, 1983; Gunderson, Maesch, & Rees, 1988; Maker, 1977; Whitmore & Maker, 1985). They may have sloppy handwriting or disruptive behaviors that make it difficult for them to complete work, and they often seem confused about their inability to perform school tasks. They show symptoms of stress; they may feel discouraged, frustrated, rejected, helpless, or isolated. They may be very skilled at intellectualization as a means of coping with their feelings of inadequacy. They are often impatient and critical and react stubbornly to criticism.

Strategies for parents

Recognize the potential and difficulty of the child. Explain the behavior of the child at school. Provide compensatory and enrichment activities.

Strategies for teachers

Provide any resources that are needed, including alternative learning experiences. Focus on their weaknesses and on their strengths or talents at the same time.

Type 6

The autonomous learners have learnt to work effectively in the school system. They are very successful, liked by parents, teachers, and peers, and have a high self-concept with some leadership capacity within their surroundings. They accept themselves and are risk takers, which goes well with their independent and self-directed nature. They feel secure designing their own educational and personal goals. They accept themselves and are able to take risks. They are also able to express their feelings, goals, and needs freely and appropriately. Few gifted children demonstrate this style at a very early age, although parents may see evidence of the style at home.

Strategies for parents

Provide opportunities for your child to explore their passions. Allow your child to be friends with people of all ages.

Strategies for teachers

Allow acceleration or enrichment. Allow students to study subjects in-depth.

In general, Types 1 and 6 are easily identifiable, at school and at home, while the other types of gifted students are not always recognized as such or misdiagnosis is shown.

Additionally, children and youth should not be defined by any one of these categories. The behavior, feelings, and needs of gifted and talented children change frequently when they are young, but as years pass there will be fewer abrupt changes and they may settle into one or two profile areas. Understanding and recognizing these different manifestations of giftedness allows you to adopt strategies to promote a cognitive, balanced emotional development.

Betts and Neihart (1988) summarized the characteristics of each profile by identifying for each: feelings and attitudes, behaviors, needs, adult and peer perceptions of type, identification, home support, and school support (Table 1.1). It is essential that educators and parents understand the cognitive, emotional, and social needs of the gifted and talented.

Identification and assessment

Several different points of view emerge from the giftedness and gifted identification. There has not yet been an established consensus on how to best define giftedness (Pfeiffer, 2003, 2012, 2015; Silverman, 2013; Sternberg, 2018). Nevertheless, high-ability students will be identified and evaluated according to the way in which giftedness is defined and how its assessment is measured (Pfeiffer, 2013a, 2015). Traditional psychometric views of giftedness still dominate the practice landscape and emphasize high intellectual prowess, exceptional academic achievement, and even extraordinary potential to demonstrate superior performance (Pfeiffer, 2015). Instead, it would be advisable to evaluate giftedness not only as an extraordinary intellectual and academic ability but also to consider high performance capability in creativity, the arts, and leadership. The practice of identifying gifted students in schools rarely identifies other areas of giftedness. This change of perspective has already started in some international contexts (Cramer, 1991; Pfeiffer, 2003; Rosado et al., 2008) and also through the provision of tools for teachers (i.e., Gifted Rating Scales). In Italy the identification and recognition of giftedness is still not a very relevant topic, especially in schools, where gifted education has experienced insufficient support (Zanetti, 2014c). It is argued that it is one of the most critical issues to be solved before designing a program for children and their identification (Gallagher, 2003; Pfeiffer, 2002).

It therefore becomes important to recognize those students who show a significant clustering of specific learning characteristics such as language properties, computing skills, spontaneous reading, curiosity, and interests, as they may possess high potential. Therefore

Table 1.1 Types and characteristics

	TYPE 1	TYPE 2	TYPE 3	TYPE 4	TYPE 5	TYPE 6
FEELINGS AND ATTITUDES	Boredom Dependent Positive self-concept Anxious Guilty about failure Extrinsic motivation Responsible for others Diminish feelings of self and rights to their emotion Self-critical	Boredom Frustration Low self-esteem Impatient/Defensive Heightened sensitivity Uncertain about social roles	Unsure Pressured Confused Guilty Insecure Diminished feelings of self and right to their emotions	Resentment Angry Depressed Explosive Poor self-concept Defensive Burn-out	Powerless Frustrated Low self-esteem Unaware Angry	Self-confident Self-accepting Enthusiastic Accepted by others Supported Desire to know and learn Accepts failure Intrinsic motivation Personal power Accepts others
BEHAVIORS	Perfectionist High achiever Seeks teacher approval and structure Non-risk taking Does well academically	Corrects teacher Questions rules, policies Is honest, direct Has mood swings Demonstrates inconsistent work habits	Denies talent Drops out of G/T and advanced classes Resists challenges Wants to belong socially Changes friends	Has intermittent attendance Doesn't complete tasks Pursues outside interests "Spaced out" in class Is self-abusive	Demonstrates inconsistent work Seems average or below May be disruptive or acts out	Has appropriate social skill Works independently Develops own goals Follows through Works without approval

	Accepts and conforms Dependent	Has poor self-control Is creative Prefers highly active and questioning approach Stands up for convictions Is competitive		Isolates self Is creative Criticizes self and others Does inconsistent work Is disruptive, acts out Seems average or below Is defensive		Follows strong areas of passion Is creative Stands up for convictions Takes risks
NEEDS	To see deficiencies To be challenged Assertiveness skills Autonomy Help with boredom Appropriate curriculum	To be connected with others To learn tact, flexibility, self-awareness, self-control, acceptance Support for creativity Contractual systems	Freedom to make choices To be aware of conflicts Awareness of feelings Support for abilities Involvement with gifted peers Career/college info Self-acceptance	An individualized program Intense support Alternatives (separate, new opportunities) Counseling (individual, group, and family) Remedial help with skills	Emphasis on strengths Coping skills G/T support group Counseling Skill development	Advocacy Feedback Facilitation Support for risks Appropriate opportunities

(Continued)

Table 1.1 (Cont.)

	TYPE 1	TYPE 2	TYPE 3	TYPE 4	TYPE 5	TYPE 6
ADULT AND PEER PERCEPTIONS OF TYPE	Loved by teachers Admired by peers Loved and accepted by parents	Find them irritating Rebellious Engaged in power struggle See them as creative Discipline problem Peers see them as entertaining Want to change them Don't view as gifted	Viewed as leaders or unrecognized Seen as average and successful Perceived to be compliant Seen as quiet/shy Adults see them as unwilling to risk Viewed as resistive	Adults are angry with them Peers are judgmental Seen as loners, dropouts, dopers, or air heads Reject them and ridicule Seen as dangerous and rebellious	Seen as "weird" Seen as "dumb" Viewed as helpless Avoided by peers Seen as average or below in ability Perceived to require a great deal of imposed structure Seen only for the disability	Accepted by peers and adults Admired for abilities Seen as capable and responsible by parents Positive influences Successful Psychologically healthy
IDENTIFICATION	Grade point average IQ tests Teacher nominations	Peer recommendations Parent nomination Interviews Performance Recommendation from	Gifted peer nomination Home nomination Community nomination Achievement testing	Review cumulative folder Interview earlier teachers Discrepancy between IQ and demonstrated achievement	Scatter of eleven points or more on WISC or WAIS Recommendation of significant others	Grade point average Demonstrated performance Products Achievement Testing Interviews

		a significant, non-related adult Creativity Testing Teacher advocate	– IQ tests Performance Teacher advocate	incongruities and inconsistencies in performance Creativity testing Gifted peer recommendation Demonstrated performance in non-school areas	Recommendation from informed special ed teacher Interview Performance Teacher Advocate	Teacher/Peer/Parent self-nominations IQ tests Creativity Testing
HOME SUPPORT	Independence Ownership Freedom to make choices Time for personal interests Risk-taking experiences	Acceptance and understanding Allow them to pursue interest Advocate for them at school Modeling appropriate behavior Family projects	Acceptance of underground Provide college and career planning experiences Time to be with same age peers Provide gifted role models Model life-long learning Give freedom to make choice	Seek counseling for family	Recognize gifted abilities Challenge them Provide risk-taking opportunities Advocate for child at school Do family projects Seek counseling for family	Advocate for child at school and in community Provide opportunities related to passions Allow friends of all ages Remove time and space restrictions Do family projects Include child in parent's passion
SCHOOL SUPPORT		Tolerance	Recognize and properly place	Diagnostic testing	Placement in gifted program	Allow development of

(Continued)

Table 1.1 (Cont.)

	TYPE 1	TYPE 2	TYPE 3	TYPE 4	TYPE 5	TYPE 6
	Accelerated and enriched curriculum Time for personal interests Compacted learning experiences Opportunities to be with intellectual peers Development of independent learning skills In-depth studies Mentorships College and career counseling	Placement with appropriate teacher Cognitive and social skill development Direct and clear communication with child Give permission for feelings Studies in-depth Mentorships build self-esteem Behavioral contracting	Give permission to take time out from G/T classes Provide same-sex role models Continue to give college and career information	Group counseling for young students Nontraditional study skills In-depth studies Mentorships Alternative out-of-classroom learning experiences	Provide needed resources Provide alternative learning experiences Begin investigations and explorations Give time to be with peers Give individual counseling	long-term integrated plan of study Accelerated and enriched curriculum Remove time and space restrictions Compacted learning experiences with pretesting In-depth studies Mentorships College and career counseling and opportunities Dual enrollment or early admission Waive traditional school policy and regulations

An in-depth look at giftedness   29

awareness of these characteristics will help parents, teachers, and psychologists with the early identification process.

Specifically, it is important to detect the presence of certain types of behavior, such as:

- the ability to understand and use abstract symbol systems at a much younger age than usual
- early language development
- early development of a rich vocabulary
- exceptional memory
- rapid pace of learning
- ability to ask reflective and probing questions
- early development of classifying and investigating skills
- fascinated by a particular subject
- complex reasoning.

It is therefore important that these characteristics are accepted and appropriate methods of identification are adopted.

When children have outstanding potential or show advanced abilities and strengths during their early childhood years, it is necessary to provide an appropriate curriculum which is matched to their special learning needs and abilities. Very young children who can read early or display other advanced abilities need to be stimulated beyond the regular curriculum. It is also critical in the early years that positive dispositions toward learning are formed and the foundations for future academic success are established. Failure to foster productive dispositions, including habits and attitudes, and to develop a love of learning can contribute to subsequent underachievement.

Early identification will enable the school to develop appropriate, comprehensive, and challenging long-term programs for exceptionally gifted young children. Kindergarten and preprimary teachers play a critical role in this process. A secure, stimulating early childhood learning environment will help students feel safe so that they can demonstrate their advanced abilities. Early indicators which suggest further investigation can be gathered through a variety of means, including:

- teacher observations and behavioral checklists
- interactions with students
- discussions with parents/educators

It is important that in real-life contexts these children are recognized and not necessarily evaluated with diagnostic tools. This is why an evaluation can already be done by adequately trained teachers who are able to use validated checklists. Indeed, teachers who spend a lot of time with children have the opportunity to observe and interact with them and, therefore, to express valid opinions (Chekaluk & Kenny, 1993; Meisel, Bickel, Nicholson, Xue, & Atkins-Burnett, 2001; Perry & Meisels, 1996).

Teachers' point of view should be considered an important source (Davidson, 1986; Pfeiffer, 2002). The use of teacher rating scales claims a long history in the identification of gifted students (Blei & Pfeiffer, 2008).

One of the most used tools for the identification of gifted students is the Gifted Rating Scales-School Form. The Gifted Rating Scales (Pfeiffer & Jarosewich, 2003) was designed as a diagnostically appropriate instrument to assist the gifted students' identification process (Siu, 2009). The test measures teachers' perception of the student's level of academic and intellectual ability, creativity, leadership, artistic talent, and motivation.

Positive results have been yielded (Rosado, Pfeiffer, & Petscher, 2008) by original standardization data and validation analysis in different contexts as well as follow-up stories (Beretta, Pfeiffer, & Zanetti, 2014; Pfeiffer & Jarosewich, 2007; Pfeiffer, Petscher, & Kumtepe, 2008; Zanetti, 2014a) which have provided support for the reliability and validity of the GRS (Li, Pfeiffer, Petscher, Kumtepe, & Mo, 2008; Lee & Pfeiffer, 2006).

The GRS is based on a multidimensional model of giftedness that incorporates the Munich model of giftedness and talent (Ziegler & Heller, 2000) and the typology that appears in the U.S. Department of Education Report, National Excellence: A Case for Developing America's Talent (Ross, 1993). The GRS has demonstrated solid psychometric properties (Li, Pfeiffer, Petscher, Kumtepe, & Mo, 2008; Margulies & Floyd, 2004; Rosado et al., 2008; Ward, 2005).

The majority of researchers agreed that this recognition can be carried out within the school context with a diagnostic evaluation even at preschool. Many of the test authors drew upon anecdotal and personal experience as well as research. Two controversial topics in gifted assessment are the use of cutoff scores and the use of only one score (often IQ $\geq$ 130) to identify a student as gifted. It has been noted elsewhere that the use of

An in-depth look at giftedness 31

a rigid cutoff score and using only one test score in high-stakes testing is contrary to Standards for Educational and Psychological Measurement (AERA, APA, & NCMEAREA, 2014) and best practices in gifted assessment (Pfeiffer, 2015; Thompson & Morris, 2008). The use of only one test provides a rather limited sample of a youngster's ability profile and may underestimate (or overestimate) their "true" ability or potential. Standards for Educational and Psychological Measurement (AERA, APA, & NCME, 2014) tend to have rigid cutoff scores which can be seen as unethical, artificial, and almost uninterpretable. As a best practice in psychological assessment, one score should never be used as a sole criterion. Assessments should include multidomain measurements and multiple perspectives. The great majority of our test authors believe that using more than one assessment measure is the *sine qua non* of the best clinical practice. Multiple data sources from multiple perspectives are always the preferred diagnostic approach, in education as well as medicine and other fields. Information from teacher rating scales, parent reports, classroom artifacts, and observations provides a more comprehensive and in-depth viewpoint (Pfeiffer, 2015).

Another controversy in the gifted field has to do with the re-evaluation of gifted students (Pfeiffer, 2013b, 2015). The majority of our text authors contend that re-evaluation is important and necessary. We find this result gratifying, as in our research lab we have found that giftedness is not only a social construct but also a fluid and dynamic construct that can often change over time. Although IQ is a fairly stable construct, a gifted student's cognitive ability profile can change over time, and for many students it can significantly change (Lohman & Korb, 2006; McCall, Appelbaum, & Hogarty, 1973; Nisbett, 2009). Re-evaluation provides an opportunity to monitor student progress, determine to what extent the student is benefiting from the special gifted program, and inform teachers if adjustments to the curriculum or instructions are prudent. Pfeiffer (2015) has argued that gifted re-evaluation should follow the same procedures as re-evaluation in special education.

One still unanswered question to which our text authors offered a variety of opinions is the frequency of gifted re-evaluation. Opinions on its frequency varied from every year to every four years. Pfeiffer (2015) suggested that the frequency of re-testing should be guided by chronological age/developmental considerations (more frequent for younger students) and the nature of the assessment (initial identification vs. grade acceleration determination vs. measuring change in a student's ability profile vs. assessing non-cognitive factors such as social competence, passion for learning, and motivation). The majority of researchers agree that it was not prudent to use rigid cutoff scores, only one test in gifted assessment, and not to conduct re-evaluations. However, there is still no full agreement on the matter. We find that the most efficient results occur with a holistic, multi-perspective assessment and best practices in gifted identification.

Until recently, identification and evaluation have privileged tools that focus on cognitive aspects, specifically the Cattell–Horn–Carroll (CHC) theory[1] (Flanagan & Harrison, 2005; Horn & Cattell, 1966) that is also expanding the hierarchical conception of intelligence and has not overcome the hierarchical aspect of intelligence, considering a multidimensionality of the aspects that make up giftedness.

A particularly interesting finding is that many leading tests used in gifted identification were not developed with the gifted population in mind. If even a few widely used tests were not developed based on a clearly articulated conceptualization of giftedness, then practitioners using these tests may miss assessing important relevant constructs to the gifted student. For example, a growing number of authorities in the gifted field contend that giftedness is multidimensional and should reflect the dynamic, developmental transformation of gifts over time (Pfeiffer, 2003; Subotnik, 2003, 2015; Subotnik, Olszewski-Kubilius, & Worrell, 2011).

Gifted evaluators, in the future, will want to measure constructs which are not typically found on many of today's most widely used tests. For example, there is a growing interest in ways to reliably and efficiently measure creativity, emotional intelligence, passion for learning, task commitment, leadership, mind-set, and potential to learn (Pfeiffer, 2015; Siegle & Langley, 2015).

An assessment of the creative dimension is certainly an area to be pursued, even if it is not yet a consolidated practice; some authors suggest it is crucial (McClain & Pfeiffer, 2012). Researchers agree that there is a necessity to identify gifted subjects early to allow them to have a more favorable development. The IQ identification is still considered controversial, especially

An in-depth look at giftedness   33

for its cutoff rigidity which does not always take into account all of the potentials. Its ability to create a profile may underestimate (or overestimate) the person's "true" ability or potential.

Twice exceptionality or misdiagnosis?

In some cases giftedness also includes critical issues or disabilities. It becomes important to recognize both these conditions in order to offer the right support to the person.

Gifted students with learning disabilities are a unique subgroup of students who demonstrate both superior intellectual ability and specific learning problems. Also known as "twice exceptional" and "dually exceptional", gifted students with learning disabilities have cognitive, psychological, and academic needs that appear distinct from those of either gifted populations or those with learning disabilities (Crawford & Snart, 1994). Twice-exceptional students tend to fall into two categories: (a) those with mild disabilities whose gifts generally mask their disabilities and (b) those whose disabilities are so severe that they mask the gift (Baum & Owen, 2004). Often these students are not identified for either gifted or special education services because of the combination of their advanced capabilities and difficulties. High intellectual functioning often compensates for the learning difficulty, obscuring both the gifted potential and the learning disability (Baum, 1990; Baum, Olenchak, & Owen, 1998). In essence, the gift masks the disability, and the disability masks the gift.

Some characteristics of giftedness can often be confused with maladaptive behaviors, even by psychologists, particularly when the levels of emotional, imaginational, intellectual, sensual, and psychomotor excitability are higher than normal. Gifted children and adults have a finely tuned psychological structure and an organized awareness, and that is why they experience life differently and more intensely than those around them.

These characteristics, however, are frequently perceived by psychotherapists and others as evidence of a mental disturbance. These characteristics can be found in gifted individuals. Gifted individuals are generally emotionally and personally vulnerable to a variety of unique relationship difficulties at home, work, school, and in the community because what they consider as normal is most often labeled as neurosis among the general population.

Gifted individuals function with relatively high levels of intensity and sensitivity, when they seek therapy they are frequently misdiagnosed because specialists receive no specialized training in the identification and treatment of the person's development.

The assessment of gifted people with asynchronous development, heightened levels of awareness, energy and emotional response, and an intense level of inner turmoil in their developmental transition is mislabeled with a personality or attentional disorder: histrionic, dysthymic, cyclothymic, borderline, narcissistic, ADHD (Attention Deficit Hyperactivity Disorder), or ADD (Attention Deficit Disorder). These are a few of the diagnostic labels mistakenly used to describe normative stages of positive disintegration. The results of this type of misdiagnosis can range from being neglected to misguiding counseling strategies that invalidate and attempt to "normalize" the complex inner process of the gifted individuals. It is extremely dangerous to misdiagnose gifted clients as they might be prescribed with medication to suppress the "symptoms of giftedness". This would neutralize the wonderful inner fury of the gifted, thus minimizing the potential for a life of accomplishment and fulfillment. As a result, they are those who are the least likely to get adequate responses to their needs.

Practical suggestions

What can a parent do for their gifted child?

Recognize the signals of high potential

Sometimes the parent may observe signs of precociousness in their child (e.g., in reading or writing, advanced vocabulary, heightened sensitivity, remarkable memory, and rapid learning) or out-of-the-norm behavior (e.g., sensibility or perfectionism). Parents do not often ask for information for fear of labeling their child or to avoid social confrontation with other parents. In these cases, however, early recognition of these signals is necessary in order to activate early support interventions and high potential evaluation.

An in-depth look at giftedness   35

Evaluate potential and risks

It is important to carry out an evaluation with a professional who can identify the potential and the risk factors of the child. The assessment is multidimensional and can involve the child, parents, and teachers. During the assessment the professional (child neuropsychiatrist, psychologist, or psychotherapist) can use direct tools (e.g., IQ assessment) or indirect tools (e.g., checklist for parents and teachers) in order to collect the child's data on cognitive, emotional, and social skills.

Share information

Once the child's giftedness has been ascertained, the parent can share this information with the child and the teachers in order to activate a support network for the child's growth. It is never functional to keep hidden information in these cases. It's also helpful to talk to parents who are "in this together" as you are. Other parents of gifted students can be an invaluable resource.

Activate support

According to the lines that emerged from the evaluation, parents have the task of supporting the child by activating care services. High-potential children may have social and emotional needs (e.g., art therapy, psychomotor, psychological support, psychotherapy) and/or scholastic (e.g., acceleration, compaction of the curriculum).

Look for extracurricular programs for gifted children

Most of the time schools can only offer limited resources to gifted children. There are many websites that provide international programs (NAGC or SENG), activities, and other resources of support for gifted students. If your country does not offer specific programs, it is still possible to identify useful extracurricular activities. In this case it is always better for parents to choose activities that do not enhance what is taught in school in order to avoid widening the gap between the student and their classmates.

Note

1 The Cattell-Horn-Carroll (CHC) theory of cognitive abilities is the most comprehensive and empirically supported psychometric theory of the structure of cognitive abilities to date. It represents the integrated works of Cattell, Horn, and Carroll. It is based on an enormous body of research on the development of intelligence and on neurocognitive basis and it is used extensively as the foundation for selecting, organizing, and interpreting tests of intelligence and cognitive abilities Most recently, it has been used for classifying intelligence and achievement batteries and neuropsychological tests to: (a) facilitate interpretation of cognitive performance; and (b) provide a foundation for organizing assessments for individuals suspected of having a learning disability. Additionally, CHC theory is the foundation on which most new and recently revised intelligence batteries are based.

References

Aderholt-Elliott, M. (1989). Perfectionism and underachievement. *Gifted Child Today*, 12, 19–21.

Angoff, W. H. (1988). The nature-nurture debate, aptitudes, and group differences. *American Psychologist*, 43(9), 713.

AERA, APA, & NCMEAREA. (2014). *Standards for educational and psychological testing*. Washington, DC: American Educational Research Association.

Baum, A. (1990). Stress, intrusive imagery, and chronic distress. *Health Psychology*, 9(6), 653.

Baum, S. M., & Owen, S. V. (2004). *To be gifted and learning disabled: Strategies for helping bright students with learning and attention difficulties*. Waco, TX: Prufrock Press Incorporated.

Baum, S. M., Olenchak, F. R., & Owen, S. V. (1998). Gifted students with attention deficits: Fact and/or fiction? Or, can we see the forest for the trees? *Gifted Child Quarterly*, 42(2), 96–104.

Beretta, A. Z. M. (2013). Metacognizione, obiettivi di apprendimento e successo scolastico in studenti ad alto potenziale della scuola superior. *Ricerche di Psicologia*, N° 2, Franco Angeli Editore, 353–370.

Beretta, A., Pfeiffer, S. I., & Zanetti, M. A. (2014). Validation of Italian version of Gifted Rating Scales-School form – preliminary data. 17–20 September: Paper ECHA 14th International Conference Ljubljana.

Betts, G. T., & Neihart, M. (1988). Profiles of the gifted and talented. *Gifted Child Quarterly*, 32(2), 248–253.

Blei, S., & Pfeiffer, S. I. (2008). Gifted identification beyond the IQ test: Rating scales and other assessment procedures. In S. I. Pfeiffer (Ed.), *Handbook of giftedness in children* (pp. 177–198). New York, NY: Springer.

Borland, J. H. (2005). Gifted education without gifted children. In R. Sternberg & J. Davidson (Eds.), *Conceptions of giftedness* (pp. 1–19). Cambridge: Cambridge University Press. doi: 10.1017/ CBO9780511610455.002.

Chekaluk, D. T., & Kenny, E. (1993). Early reading performance: A comparison of teacher-based and test-based assessments. *Journal of Learning Disabilities*, 26(4), 227–236.

Clark, B. (1992). *Growing up gifted.* New York, NY: Macmillan.

Cramer, R. (1991). The education of gifted children in the United States: A Delphi study. *Gifted Child Quarterly*, 35, 84–91.

Crawford, S., & Snart, F. (1994). Process-based remediation of decoding in gifted LD students: Three case studies. *Roeper Review*, 16(4), 247–252.

Dabrowski, K. (1964). *Positive disintegration.* Oxford: Little, Brown.

Dąbrowski, K., & Piechowski, M. M. (1977). *Theory of levels of emotional development: From primary integration to self-actualization.* Vol. 2. Oceanside, NY: Dabor Science Publications.

Daniels, P. (1983). *Teaching the gifted/learning disabled child.* Rockville, MD: Aspen Systems Corporation.

Davidson, J. E. (1986). The role of insight in giftedness. In R. J. Sternberg & J. E. Davidson (Eds.), *Conceptions of giftedness* (pp. 201–222). New York: Cambridge University Press.

European Commission (2006). *Commission staff working paper: Progress towards the common objectives in education and training indicators and benchmarks.* Brussels: European Commission.

Feldhusen, J. F. (1995). Creativity: A knowledge base, metacognitive skills, and personality factors. *The Journal of Creative Behavior*, 29(4), 255–268.

Flanagan, D. P., & Harrison, P. L. (2005). *Contemporary intellectual assessment* (2nd ed.). New York, NY: Guilford.

Fox, L. H., Brody, L., & Tobin, D. (1983). *Learning-disabled/gifted children.* Baltimore, MD: University Park Press.

Gagné, F. (1985). Giftedness and talent: Reexamining a reexamination of the definitions. *Gifted Child Quarterly*, 29(3), 103–112.

Gagné, F. (1995). From giftedness to talent: A developmental model and its impact on the language of the field. *Roeper Review*, 18, 103–111.

Gagné, F. (2000). Understanding the complex choreography of talent development through DMGT-based analysis. In K. A. Heller, F. J. Mönks, R. J. Sternberg, & R. F. Subotnik (Eds.), *International handbook of giftedness and talent* (pp. 67–80). Oxford: Elsevier Science.

Gagné, F. (2003). Transforming gifts into talents: The DMGT as a developmental theory. In N. Colangelo & G. A. Davis (Eds.), *Handbook of gifted education*, 3rd ed. (pp. 60–74). Boston, MA: Allyn & Bacon.

38 Maria Assunta Zanetti

Gagné, F. (2004). Transforming gifts into talents: The DMGT as a developmental theory. *High Ability Studies*, 15, 119–147. http://dx.doi.org/10.1080/1359813042000314682.

Gagné, F. (2009). Building gifts into talents: Detailed overview of the DMGT 2.0. In B. MacFarlane & T. Stambaugh (Eds.), *Leading change in gifted education: The festschrift of Dr. Joyce VanTassel-Baska*. Waco, TX: Prufrock Press.

Gagné, F. (2013). The DMGT: Changes within, beneath, and beyond. *Talent Development & Excellence*, 5(1), 5–19.

Gagné, F., & Guenther, Z. (2010). O DMGT 2.0 de Françoys Gagné: Construindotalentos a partir da dotação *Sobredotação*, 11, 7–23.

Gallagher, J. J. (2003). Issues and challenges in the education of gifted students. *Handbook of Gifted Education*, 3, 11–23.

Gallagher, J. (2008). Psychology, psychologists, and gifted students. In S. I. Pfeiffer (Ed.), *Handbook of giftedness in children* (pp. 1–12). New York, NY: Springer.

Gardner, H. (1993). *Multiple intelligences*. New York, NY: Basic Books.

Gardnerd, H. (1983). *Frames of mind: The theory of multiple intelligences*. London: Heinemann.

George, P. (1992). *How to untrack your school*. Alexandria, VA: Association for Supervision and Curriculum Development.

Guilford, J. P. (1950). Creativity. *American Psychologist*, 5, 444–454.

Gunderson, C. W., Maesch, C., & Rees, J. W. (1988). The gifted/learning disabled student. *Gifted Child Quarterly*, 31, 158–160.

Hollingworth, L. S. (1926). *Gifted children*. New York, NY: Macmillan.

Hollingworth, L. S. (1942). *Children above 180 IQ: Stanford-Binet*. New York, NY: World Book, Yonkers-on-Hudson.

Horn, J. L., & Cattell, R. B. (1966). Refinement and test of the theory of fluid and crystallized general intelligences. *Journal of Educational Psychology*, 57(5), 253.

Kaufman, J. C., & Plucker, J. A. (2011). Intelligence and creativity. In R. J. Sternberg & S. B. Kaufman (Eds.), *The Cambridge handbook of intelligence* (pp. 771–783). Cambridge: Cambridge University Press.

Kaufman, J. C., Plucker, J. A., & Baer, J. (2008). *Essentials of creativity assessment*. Vol. 53. New York: John Wiley & Sons.

Kerr, B. (1985). Smart girls, gifted women: Special guidance concerns. *Roeper Review*, 8(1), 30–31.

Kerr, H. T. (1991). From here to there. *Theology Today*, 48(3), 265–268. https://doi.org/10.1177/004057369104800301.

Lee, D., & Pfeiffer, S. I. (2006). The reliability and validity of a Korean-translated version of the Gifted Ratings Scales. *Journal of Psychoeducational Assessment*, 24, 210–224.

An in-depth look at giftedness   39

Li, H., Pfeiffer, S. I., Petscher, Y., Kumtepe, A. T., & Mo, G. (2008). Validation of the Gifted Rating Scales-School form in China. *Gifted Child Quarterly*, 52(2), 160–169.

Lohman, D. F. (2009). Identifying academically talented students: Some general principles, two specific procedures. In L. V. Shavinina (Ed.), *International handbook of giftedness* (pp. 971–997). New York, NY: Springer Science.

Lohman, D. F., & Korb, K. A. (2006). Gifted today but not tomorrow? Longitudinal changes in ability and achievement during elementary school. *Journal for the Education of the Gifted*, 29(4), 451–484.

Maker, J. (1977). *Providing programs for the gifted handicapped*. Reston, VA: Council for Exceptional Children.

Margulies, A., & Floyd, R. (2004). Book review: Gifted Rating Scales (GRS). *Journal of Psychoeducational Assessment*, 22(3), 275–282.

McCall, R. B., Appelbaum, M. I., & Hogarty, P. S. (1973). Developmental changes in mental performance. *Monographs of the Society for Research in Child Development*, 38, 1–84.

McClain, M. C., & Pfeiffer, S. I. (2012). Identification of gifted students in the United States today: A look at state definitions, policies, and practices. *Journal of Applied School Psychology*, 28(1), 59–88.

Neihart, M. (1999). The impact of giftedness on psychological well-being. *Roeper Review*, 22(1), 10–17.

Neihart, M., Reis, S. M., Robinson, N. M., & Moon, S. M. (2002). *The social and emotional development of gifted children: What do we know?* Waco, TX: Prufrock Press.

Nisbett, R. E. (2009). *Intelligence and how to get it: Why schools and cultures count*. New York, NY: Norton.

Perry, N. E., & Meisels, S. J. (1996). *How accurate are teacher judgments of students' academic performance?* Working Paper Series.

Pfeiffer, S. I. (2002). Identifying gifted and talented students: Recurring issues and promising solutions. *Journal of Applied School Psychology*, 1, 31–50.

Pfeiffer, S. I. (2003). Challenges and opportunities for students who are gifted: What the experts say. *Gifted Child Quarterly*, 47, 161–169.

Pfeiffer, S. I. (2012). Current perspectives on the identification and assessment of gifted students. *Journal of Psychoeducational Assessment*, 30, 3–9.

Pfeiffer, S. I. (2013a). Lessons learned from working with high-ability students. *Gifted Education International*, 29(1), 86–97.

Pfeiffer, S. I. (2013b). *Serving the gifted*. New York, NY: Routledge.

Pfeiffer, S. I. (2015). *Essentials of gifted assessment*. Hoboken, NJ: Wiley.

Pfeiffer, S. I., & Jarosewich, T. (2003). *Gifted Rating Scales*. San Antonio, TX: The Psychological Corporation.

Pfeiffer, S. I., & Jarosewich, I. (2007). The Gifted Rating Scales-School Form: An analysis of the standardization sample based on age, gender, race, and diagnostic efficiency. *Gifted Child Quarterly*, 51, 39–50.

Pfeiffer, S. I., Petscher, Y., & Kumtepe, A. (2008). The Gifted Rating Scales-School Form: A validation study based on age, gender, and race. *Roeper Review*, 30(2), 140–146.

Piechowski, M. M. (1999). Overexcitabilities. In M. A. Piechowski (Ed.), *Encyclopedia of creativity*, Vol. 2 (pp. 325–334). San Diego, CA: Academic Press.

Plomin, R. (1998). Genetic influence and cognitive abilities. *Behavioral and Brain Sciences*, 21, 420–421.

Powell, P. M., & Haden, T. (1984). The intellectual and psychosocial nature of extreme giftedness. *Roeper Review*, 6(3), 131–133.

Renati, R., & Zanetti, M. A. (2012). L'universo poco conosciuto della plusdotazione. *Psicologia e Scuola* n. 23. Giunti, 18–24.

Renzulli, J. S. (1994). *Schools for talent development: A practical plan for total school improvement*. Mansfield Center, CT: Creative Learning Press.

Robinson, N. M., & Noble, K. (1991). Social-emotional development and adjustment of gifted children. In M. C. Wang, M. C. Reynolds, & H. J. Walberg (Eds.), *Handbook of special education research and practice: Emerging programs: Volume 4* (pp. 57–76). New York, NY: Pergamon Press.

Rosado, J. I., Pfeiffer, S. I., & Petscher, Y. (2008). The reliability and validity of a Spanish translated version of the gifted rating scales. *Gifted and Talented International*, 23(1), 105–114.

Ross, P. O. (1993). *National excellence: A case for developing America's talent*. Washington, DC: U.S. Government Printing Office. Superintendent of Documents Mail Stop: SSOP, 20402-9328.

Siegle, D., & Langley, S. D. (2015). Mindset. In M. Neihart, S. I. Pfeiffer, & T. L. Cross (Eds.), *The social and emotional development of gifted children*, 2nd ed. (pp. 269–281). Waco, TX: Profrock Press Incorporated.

Silverman, L. K. (2002). Asynchronous development. In M. Neihart, S. M. Reis, N. M. Robinson, & S. M. Moon (Eds.), *The social and emotional development of gifted children: What do we know?* (pp. 31–37). Waco, TX: Prufrock Press.

Silverman, L. K. (2013). Asynchronous development: Theoretical bases and current applications. In C. S. Neville, M. M. Piechowski, & S. S. Tolan (Eds.), *Off the charts: Asynchrony and the gifted child* (pp. 18–47). Unionville, NY: Royal Fireworks Press.

Simonton, D. K. (1999). Talent and its development: An emergenic and epigenetic model. *Psychological Review*, 106(3), 435–457. https://doi.org/10.1037/0033-295X.106.3.435.

Siu, A. F. (2009). Trait emotional intelligence and its relationships with problem behavior in Hong Kong adolescents. *Personality and Individual Differences*, 47, 553–557.

Smith, J. S. (2006). Examining the long-term impact of achievement loss during the transition to high school. *Journal of Secondary Gifted Education*, 17(4), 211–221.

Sternberg, R. J. (1986). *Intelligences applied*. New York, NY: Harcourt Brace Jovanovich.

Sternberg, R. J. (1991). Theory-based testing of intellectual abilities: Rationale for the triarchic, abilities test. In H. Rowe (Ed.), *Intelligence: Reconceptualization and measurement* (pp. 183–202). Hillsdale, NJ: Lawrence Erlbaum.

Sternberg, R. J. (2018). Theories of intelligence. In S. I. Pfeiffer, E. Shaunessy-Dedrick, & M. Foley-Nicpon (Eds.), *APA handbooks in psychology: APA handbook of giftedness and talent* (pp. 145–161). Washington, D.C.: American Psychological Association. http://dx.doi.org/10.1037/0000038-010.

Sternberg, R. J., & Davidson, J. E. (2005). *Conceptions of giftedness*. Cambridge: Cambridge University Press.

Strang, R. (1965). The psychology of the gifted child. In W. B. Barbe (Ed.), *Psychology and education of the gifted: Selected readings* (pp. 113–117). New York, NY: Appleton-Century-Crofts.

Subotnik, R. F. (2003). A developmental view of giftedness: From being to doing. *Roeper Review*, 26(1), 14–15.

Subotnik, R. F. (2015). Psychosocial strength training: The missing piece in talent development. *Gifted Child Today*, 38(1), 41–48.

Subotnik, R. F., Olszewski-Kubilius, P., & Worrell, F. C. (2011). Rethinking giftedness and gifted education: A proposed direction forward based on psychological science. *Psychological Science in the Public Interest*, 12(1), 3–54.

Terman, L. M. (1925). *Mental and physical traits of a thousand gifted children: Genetic studies of genius*. Volume 1. Stanford, CA: Stanford University Press.

Terrassier, J.-C. (1985). Dyssynchrony: Uneven development. In J. Freeman (Ed.), *The psychology of gifted children* (pp. 265–274). New York: John Wiley.

Terrassier, J.-C. (2004). *Les enfants surdoués ou la précocité embarrassante*, 6th edition. Issy-les-Moulineaux: ESF.

Thompson, K. C., & Morris, R. J. (2008). To gifted students. In S. I. Pfeiffer (Ed.), *Handbook of giftedness in children: Psychoeducational theory, research, and best practices* (pp. 309–326). Tallahassee, FL: Springer.

Tieso, C. L. (2007). Patterns of overexcitability. *Roeper Review*, 24(4), 232–237.

Torrance, E. P. (1967). *Understanding the fourth grade slump in creative thinking*. Final Report. Athens, GA: The University of Georgia.

VanTassel-Baska, J. (1998). *Excellence in educating gifted & talented learners*. Denver, CO: Love Publishing Company.

Ward, S. A. (2005). Review of Gifted Rating Scales. In R. A. Spies & B. S. Plake (Eds.), *The sixteenth mental measurements yearbook* (pp. 404–407). Lincoln, NE: Buros Institute of Mental Measurement of the University of Nebraska–Lincoln.

Webb, J. T., & Kleine, P. A. (1993). Assessing gifted and talented children. In J. Willis (Ed.), *Testing young children* (pp. 383–407). Austin, TX: Pro-Ed.

White, K., Fletcher-Campbell, F., Ridley, K., & LGA Educational Research Programme (2003). *What works for gifted and talented pupils: A review of recent research*. Slough, UK: NFER, National Foundation for Educational Research.

Whitmore, J. R. (1980). *Giftedness, conflict, and underachievement*. Boston, MA: Allyn & Bacon.

Whitmore, J. R., & Maker, J. (1985). *Intellectual giftedness in disabled persons*. Rockville, MD: Aspen Systems Corporation.

Zanetti, M. A. (2014a, 18–19 October). Plusdotazione in Italia. Strategie di individuazione dei bambini plusdotati e metodologie di inclusione dei bambini plusdotati nel contesto scolastico. *Giornate di studio LO SPORTELLO TRA I BANCHI*. Roma.

Zanetti, M. A. (2014b). Uno sguardo sui disturbi del comportamento: il caso dei bambini ad alto potenziale. In *IV Convegno nazionale Disturbi dell'apprendimento e del comportamento nella scuola digitale*. 26–27 Settembre. Roma: Lumsa.

Zanetti, M. A. (2014c). Bambini ad alto potenziale (gifted children): impariamo a riconoscerli, *QI: Questioni e Idee in psicologia*, 20 Settembre.

Ziegler, A., & Heller, K. (2000). Effects of an attribution retraining with female students gifted in physics. *Journal for the Education of the Gifted*, 23(2), 217–243.

Chapter 2

The gifted adolescent world

Maria Assunta Zanetti and Gianluca Gualdi

To be an adolescent gifted student

Adolescence has been defined as a phase of development which is characterized by temporary conflict due to the presence of biological, psychological and social pressures that, before becoming a new condition, are experienced by the subject with disharmony, as a lack of integration, as a suspension between an unused past and a just-sketched future (Erikson, 1968). The attempt to overcome confusion and ambivalence in order to establish oneself in a stable, coherent and unique way may cause an identity crisis. The emotional climate of adolescence today has radically changed because the way in which adults face parenting has changed (Charmet, 2000). There are fewer rules and regulations and more attention to support the emotional and relational growth of the child, their right to be themselves and to express their personality, following their own internal times of maturation and acquisition of social skills (Charmet, 2000). The transition from a privileged childhood to adulthood is experienced with great emotional intensity. Boredom, sadness, fear and shame alternate as capable factors of governing the behavior of children and the discomfort they experience. Moreover, today's society presents a lack of group activities, meeting places and support communities; these aspects are risk factors as the adolescent needs to belong to a group. The consequences are an increase in delinquent behavior, substance use (alcohol and drugs) and early sexualization, situations that are observed at an increasingly early age, since "positive contexts" are not available.

Giftedness can complicate the young teenager in their typical search for their true self within a period of increasing complexity.

Research (Burks, Jensen and Terman, 1930; Zanetti, 2017) suggests that feelings of loneliness and alienation, typical of this age, are more pronounced in gifted students than in their peers. Furthermore, asynchronous development is a qualitative difference that can make teenagers particularly vulnerable to social and emotional domains, thus requiring the attention of parents, teachers and consultants to ensure that optimal development occurs. Because the intensity and unpredictability of emotions can create self-management problems, it is essential to find meaning. The condition of giftedness can, therefore, involve learning difficulties and real dropout situations, thus fueling experiences of frustration, behavior problems and general malaise at school.

Gifted teenagers have the ability to experience the world from a different perspective than the norm, with qualitative differences in terms of sensitivity, intensity, idealism, perfectionism, excitement, complexity, introversion and moral concern. Sword (2001) has studied the emotional and intellectual traits and social characteristics of "gifted" teenagers, highlighting that they not only think differently from their peers, but also perceive things differently. These differences in sensitivity can be explained in terms of intensity, awareness and intuition.

The difficulty in building a social network often appears in the early years of primary school, but it becomes an important risk factor in adolescence. In fact, the adolescent lacking a social support network has a high probability of developing a mood disorder or deviant behavior such as delinquent conduct, abuse or behavior that exceeds the limit or goes against the rules (Pfeiffer and Stocking, 2000).

The literature concerning gender differences among gifted adolescents is quite large. Not everyone agrees with Hedges and Nowell (1995) or with Benbow and colleagues (2000), who support the existence of significant differences between the innate abilities of gifted teenagers.

Indeed, Golombok and Fivush (1994) discuss how "accurate statistical analysis through hundreds of studies has shown that gender differences in mathematical and linguistic skills are so small that they can be considered practically non-existent" (p. 177). They concluded that "gender differences measured in attitudes were the result of a complex interaction between small biological differences and large gender differences in socialization experiences" (p. 176). In addition, Heller (2000), in an international review on gender differences,

The gifted adolescent world   45

identified how female adolescents with high potential were more influenced by social pressures compared to males. Non-recognition and exploitation of high potential can lead to the development of negative consequences such as boredom, underachievement and sub-learning with a high probability of developing frustration, low motivation, low self-esteem, and emotional, social and behavioral problems (Neihart et al., 2002). Innate perfectionism could cause gifted adolescents' self-esteem to drop.

High-potential students are able to compensate their difficulty in facing complex challenges during primary school years by getting good grades but might feel unprepared as they continue with their education (Zanetti et al., 2016). Long-life choices are crucial for high-potential students. Multiple potentials lead to multiple career choices. At the same time, potentials are not always connected to real skills, and when this aspect emerges the students feel a sense of indecision and impotence in facing a path, which might demotivate them. The expectation of parents or teachers is significant as they observe cognitive abilities that they would like to see realized and concretized in a job or in a positive educational path, but that the student cannot always put into play. In some cases, parents' expectations can also create anxiety, influence perfectionism or be very different from those of the student.

High-potential students also have the characteristic of being multi-faceted. The idea that they can become whatever they wish turns into a dilemma when making a choice because there is no school or profession that fully responds to their interests, skills or values that they present. This aspect is observed in the various extracurricular activities that these students often perform simultaneously, frequently changing them when they no longer perceive a sense of growth or motivation.

It is commonly thought that high cognitive abilities correlate with a certain future, multiple possibilities, insured successes, well-defined objectives and autonomy in choices. In reality, high-potential students are a heterogeneous group and as such they each have different characteristics and trajectories: some students are sensation seekers and experience different activities and behaviors even without the certainty of success; moreover, like all students, this type also has limited resources and experiences, which can be promoted, but which do not allow them to cover any educational and/or professional career.

High-potential students are perceived as not in need of help and this aspect becomes an idea of the children themselves, who tend to ask less for support services within the school because they believe they are there for those with learning difficulties or poor cognitive skills.

It is therefore essential to be able to support and help high-potential students to understand and address their intellectual, social and emotional needs in order to promote awareness of their potential, developing a realistic self-concept. This aspect integrates the observation of one's strengths related to those of weakness, which is a systemic vision and an integrated vision of oneself.

During the different stages of development, different areas of promotion of the student's competences come into play, particularly during primary school when it is useful to promote self-awareness, one's own interests and the aspirations of life. It may be useful to promote recognition of the professions' social values and the influences of desires which critically assess parental expectations. During the first level of secondary school the topic of students' search for their identity becomes important. This is done by favoring the continuous construction of self-awareness and looking for professions which are in relation to their aspirations and expectations. In fact, it becomes very important to understand individual jobs in their role, materials and actions which require effort and promote the identification of the ideal training/professional path for each individual. In the secondary school stage, independence and decision making become key issues for the transition from adolescent to adult. This aspect is connected to the identification of the possible congruences between a professional future and lifestyle.

With high-potential students, the role of teachers and parents that encourage and foster group experience, internships and supervised traineeships becomes fundamental in order to provide situations in which to experiment actively and directly and in which commitment and consistency can be proven on the field. Particular attention should be paid to female students who often experience greater pressure to make specific choices because of the persistence of gender stereotypes (Reis, 2002).

Risk factors

Potential is interpretable as a continuum between resource and risk. Much depends on the personal characteristics of the student,

The gifted adolescent world 47

their life contexts and the experiences they face during growth and adolescence. Having a high IQ is not necessarily related to successful schooling. Some believe that this population is advantaged to the point of not needing specific interventions.

On a psychological level, high-potential students often refer to a sense of diversity from chronological-age peers, with difficulty in understanding some peculiar characteristics, and problems in the development of the self and one's own identity. Not recognizing and exploiting the potential of these youngsters, particularly in the school context, can lead them to feel unrecognized and misunderstood, with a sense of boredom and frustration, which are aspects related to the phenomenon of underachieving (sub-learning) and school dropouts. These phenomena particularly emerge in lower secondary school and upper secondary school when changes related to adolescence come into play. Students in such situations tend to develop frustration, low motivation, low self-esteem, and emotional, social and behavioral problems (Moon and Reis, 2004). These aspects, in relation to self-directed or socially prescribed perfectionism, strongly influence self-perception with a tendency to a good level of self-esteem but poor self-efficacy. In fact, these young people report that they feel "potentially able to give much more than what they do", with the recognition of skills that they do not seem able to exploit (Gualdi et al., 2016a).

Many risk factors emerge that underlie the difficulties of high-potential students. These aspects can arise as individuals, in the family context or in the social context.

Another important psychological aspect is introversion, a characteristic trait of personality, with which the adolescent is led to close themselves in their inner world out of shyness and could be rather wary or hostile in human contacts and social relationships. This aspect can cause feelings of loneliness and can therefore influence social development. Since the end of the 1990s, a particular psychological condition has been described in Japan for which the term "Hikikomori" is used. It literally means "social withdrawal" (Saito, 1998), which identifies a particular group of adolescents or young adults who withdraw from social life and who tend not to have relationships outside the family (Saito, 1998; Zielenziger, 2008). This condition is observed with school absence frequencies, for a prolonged period of at least 6 months, and a lack of relationships, with the exception of those with the closest family members (Saito, 1998). With the persistence of this condition we can see how the Hikikomori come to abandon school and friends, interrupting every kind of communication and living long periods in isolation (Ricci, 2008); they show their discomfort by remaining within the walls of their home, going out only at night or early in the morning (that is, in those moments when they are certain of not meeting people they know) or pretending to go to school or work and instead wandering aimlessly for the entire day (Saito, 1998). This phenomenon is frequently related to Internet addiction; that is, to Internet dependency (Wong, 2015). It is in fact possible that the state of isolation pushes the Hikikomori to seek refuge in the network and to use it as a means of contact with the outside world (Ricci, 2011); they often play role-playing games online for many hours, creating an avatar that represents them and allowing them to experience successful relationships, without having to present themselves for what they really are. Use of the Internet, however, seems to represent a consequence and not a cause of social isolation (Ricci, 2011). Some studies show that most of the boys identified as Hikikomori have high cognitive abilities and frequently result in not previously identified high-potential students.

The term self-efficacy refers to the trust that each person has in their ability to obtain the desired effects with their actions. In particular, according to Ricci (2011), the sense of self-efficacy corresponds to the beliefs about one's ability to organize and execute the sequences of actions needed to produce certain results. For example, if self-efficacy is low, the adolescent believes that their actions rarely achieve the desired results, and consequently they will choose easily achievable goals that guarantee low commitment to their realization in order to avoid high levels of stress. Self-efficacy plays a crucial role in school performance where it is often confused with self-esteem. In reality, according to Bandura, self-efficacy is a personal capacity, while self-esteem is a value judgment on oneself; they are therefore interrelated aspects, but not dependent on each other.

Self-injury is defined as a behavior aimed at damaging oneself and can include cuts of the skin, scratches, self-inflicted burns, as well as tearing off hair or ingesting poisons, drugs or objects (Hawton, Saunders and O'Connor, 2012), all actions that are characterized by the intentionality to hurt oneself (Cross, 2007). Society holds a taboo about self-injurious behavior, therefore self-inflicted injuries are generally hidden (Cross, 2007). Despite the

The gifted adolescent world   49

difficulties in accurately assessing the size of the phenomenon, it is estimated that about 10% of adolescents have experienced at least one act of self-harm (Hawton, Saunders and O'Connor, 2012) and according to Barton-Breck and Heyman (2012) the prevalence rates of self-harm among boys vary from 5% to 6%. A review carried out by Klonsky and Muehlenkamp (2007) examines the main theories that explain the reasons why adolescents resort to self-harm. The first, and also the most common, is the regulation of distress and anxiety (Klonsky and Muehlenkamp, 2007); the behavior of cutting oneself is carried out by the gifted teenager as a strategy to alleviate pain, which is often kept to oneself and not shared (Cross, 2007). Fox and Hawton (2004) have noted that, in fact, cutting oneself is an effort to get relief from tension, thoughts and emotions and helps the individual regain a sense of control (Fox and Hawton, 2004), even if in a dysfunctional way. A model proposed by Chapman and collaborators focuses on the idea that self-injurious gestures are reiterated to try to extinguish unwanted "psychological states" (Chapman, Gratz and Brown, 2006), typical of gifted teenagers. It could therefore be said that the implementation of self-injurious behavior is a transformation into physical suffering, and therefore it is real and more easily manageable compared to internal, emotional suffering that one does not know how to control; inflicting pain and the sight of one's own blood allows one to have tangible proof that one's suffering is real and there is something concrete and visible for which one feels pain. Another reading is that the implementation of such conduct is aimed at self-punishment or as a form of self-directed rage (Nock et al., 2008; Hooley and St Germain, 2013), suggesting that there is a relationship between self-criticism and self-harm. Other reasons that encourage adolescents to such gestures can be: to realize uncontrollable feelings in trying to know themselves, or to fill the internal void with external, physical, real, quantifiable and controllable pain (Rossi Monti and D'Agostino, 2009), to punish, extirpate or modify the "bad" part of oneself (Haas and Popp, 2006), and to communicate without words and to find an expressive channel for something that words cannot say in the hope of obtaining caring responses (Rossi Monti and D'Agostino, 2009). Many identified aspects, such as marked perfectionism, marked impulsivity, social isolation and dysfunctional parent–child relationships, are related to personological characteristics which predispose most subjects to suicide. It also seems that being bullied is one of the predisposing factors to consider (Hawton, Saunders and O'Connor, 2012). At the extreme margins of the continuum of a self-injurious conduct are suicidal behaviors that are less frequent than the conduct of self-harm (Muehlenkamp, 2005, 2012; Andover and Gibb, 2010). However, studies carried out on these topics underline how self-injurious behaviors are considered to be risk factors for suicide (Asarnow, Porta and Spirito, 2011; Guan, Fox and Prinstein, 2012; Wilkinson and Goodyer, 2011).

The asynchrony of development that may characterize some high-potential adolescents may not be dysfunctional at times when the social, family and school environment encompasses the needs and peculiarities of the individual. In fact, high-potential students frequently present specific needs on the cognitive, social and emotional level (VanTassel-Baska, 2003). The possibility of emotional and behavioral problems is frequent if this process does not emerge. Therefore, the family, understood as the primary context of development of the child, and the parent–child relationship play a fundamental role in the development and growth of the individual. In particular, the relationship between adult and minor is not univocal but bidirectional, and in this mutual interaction the personality, psychological resources of the parents and characteristics of the children (Belsky, 1984), but also the culture and contexts of belonging, play a fundamental role (Bornstein, 2002; Baiocco and Laghi, 2009). If we consider a limited parenting style, we might come across risks in the parent–child relationship. The child cannot only be considered as the product of parents' methods of taking care of the offspring (Baumrind, 1971). Being parents of teenagers is a complex task, but being parents of high-potential individuals has been defined as a challenging educational task (May, 2000). When they are underage they may present socio-emotional needs that, combined with a sometimes difficult temperament, can lead parents to experience stress and a sense of impotence (Silverman, 1998). Parents frequently find themselves unprepared and in difficulty in managing the sensitivity and intensity of their children, failing to provide them with real emotional containment and regulation (Pfeiffer and Stocking, 2000; Morawska and Sanders, 2009). Often the characteristics of high-potential adolescents are not fully understood even by mental health and psychological specialists, which makes it even more difficult for parents to identify child support and support strategies (Hartnett, Nelson and Rinn,

The gifted adolescent world 51

2004; Rinn and Reynolds, 2012). Studies showed that high-potential children can meet two main difficulties. A personal problem could be excessive self-criticism and the fear of taking risks which can impact on the exploration of the environment. An environmental problem could be the difficulty of conforming to the norms or the scholastic culture.

When personal or environmental problems are present, the activation of family support is useful, which can help reduce the "scholastic disaffection", the development of dysfunctional behaviors and/or trajectories of maladaptive development (Jolly and Matthews, 2012). This aspect is crucial when we observe how family values, traditions and expectations are fundamental for the development of talent (Olszewski, Kulieke and Buescher, 1987; Kulieke and Olszewski-Kubilius, 1989); this is why there are many studies that have attempted to examine the characteristics of "gifted" adolescent families (Colangelo and Dettmann, 1983; Friedman and Rogers, 1998; Moon, Jurich and Feldhusen, 1996). What emerges from these studies is that high potential is expressed in a performance only if the living environment is really supportive and promotes the implementation of its capabilities for those that are or potentially can be. An environment that is not supportive, characterized by pressure to achieve results or incompatible objectives, instead increases the risk of dysfunctional developmental trajectories or the internal rooting of potentially negative and disturbing characteristics of the individual child's well-being (e.g., socially prescribed perfectionism that influences an already high self-directed perfectionism). The ideal family environment is that which is able to provide cognitive stimuli, a point of excellence of these children, but at the same time is able to fulfill emotional and personal needs. Therefore, a high level of cohesion and mutual support within the family is to be considered a factor of protection, which at the same time encourages the independence of high-potential adolescents to a greater extent compared to parents of "non-gifted" individuals (Karnes and Shwedel, 1987).

Cornell and Grossberg (1987) have also found that family support is essential for the emotional regulation of the plus-assisted adolescent. Higher levels of cohesion and expression, and low levels of conflict in the family, have been associated with greater self-esteem, greater self-control and lower levels of anxiety for the child (Cornell and Grossberg, 1987). In support of this, several studies (Reis, Hebert, Diaz, Maxfield and Ratley, 1995) indicate that families of underdeveloped underachievers were characterized by conflicts and family instability.

The theory of Baumrind (1966) proposes three distinct prototypes of parenting: authoritarian, permissive and authoritative.

Parents who use an authoritarian style emphasize the child's control and obedience, limiting their autonomy; this parenting style has been associated with negative behavior and emotional problems in the student, such as aggression, resistance to authority, depression, low self-esteem and difficulty in making decisions (Whitfield, 1987; Forward, 1989; Baumrind, 1991; Bigner, 1994; Wenar, 1994; Carlson, Uppal and Prosser, 2000; Reitman, Rhode, Hupp and Altobello, 2002).

Parents who adopt a permissive style tend to have little expectation in their children, place few limits on their behavior and allow them to make decisions and regulate their activities (Baumrind, 1991). Gifted teenagers raised by permissive parents have poor social skills, low self-esteem and are often seen as selfish, irresponsible, spoiled, undisciplined and antisocial (Baumrind, 1991).

The common idea is that a talented child should become a successful adult. On the one hand, this statement encourages some adolescents to give their best and try, but on the other hand it can be experienced by some as a source of strong pressure, with the risk of disorientation and anxiety. A study carried out over several years by Freeman (2010) shows that only about 25% of high-potential students have obtained educational qualifications that matched what their initial premises suggested. Most of the subjects with high potential have in fact undertaken paths that are not always linear because of various factors that can be traced back to asynchrony but also to the pressure of both family and social expectations (e.g., teachers, coaches, etc.). It is therefore important that all the figures involved in the life of the adolescent with high potential do not have negative expectations which are too high or very different from those of the individual. This is also because adolescents with potential often already place high pressure on themselves to succeed in tasks or challenges. It is therefore desirable that the figures around these children tend to concentrate as little as possible on academic success alone, favoring more emotional and social goals.

A complex model for gifted adolescents

Starting from some theories of reference, we wanted to try to create a summary model of the emerging data from the literature which was reported in the previous chapter, with respect to what influences, in a more or less direct way, the development of an adolescent with high cognitive potential.

The starting point was the ecological model of Bronfenbrenner (1979), which sees the development of the individual as a series of concentric circles, linked together by relationships:

- The microsystem is the central level within which the minimal interpersonal units made up of dyads (e.g., mother–child) relate, and with other dyads with significant direct interactions.
- The mesosystem is a system of microsystems: it refers to two or more contexts in which the subject participates directly in an active way and to their interconnections.
- The exosystem consists of the interconnection between two or more social contexts, at least one of which is external to the direct action of the subject. An example of an exosystem is the relationship between a parent's family and work life.
- The macrosystem includes the political and economic institutions, the values of society and its culture: the complex beliefs and behaviors that characterize the macrosystem are transmitted from one generation to the next through socialization processes conducted by various cultural institutions, such as family, school, church, workplace and political-administrative structures.

Returning to the systems model, we started by placing the gifted teenager in the center, with a series of factors interacting with each other. In particular, the systems consist of:

- Physical factors, i.e., age and gender;
- Psychological factors, such as idealism and perfectionism, which can be self-oriented or socially prescribed, over-excitability (psychomotor, sensory, imaginative, intellectual and emotional) and traits such as introversion or extroversion and metacognition;

- Emotional factors, such as socio-emotional competence, empathy and social skills;
- Mental factors, which in turn are divided into intellectual factors, which include the nine intelligences of Gardner, memory, IQ and creativity, and into cognitive factors, among which we find cognitive styles (naturalist, bodily kinesthetic, musical, logical-mathematical, existential, interpersonal, linguistic, intra-personal, spatial);
- Transversal factors, such as self-efficacy, goal orientation and decision-making skills.

These factors are in a mutual interaction relationship and should systematically influence the performance of each gifted teenager, which is closely related to the cognitive factors and the type of gifted student.

By conditioning the performance, the combination of all these factors can contribute to the development of possible risk situations, such as:

- frustration, irritability, anxiety, boredom and social isolation
- demotivation, low self-esteem and social rejection
- difficulty with peer relationships
- loneliness, phobias, interpersonal problems, fear of failure and perfectionism
- lack of protective factors (resilience model)
- fear of failure
- depression
- poor academic performance
- leaving school

Within the microsystem there are all those interpersonal relationships, shared activities, roles and rules that mostly take place within defined places.

Examples of microsystems are:

- the family, in particular family communication, family cohesion and flexibility;
- the peer group, on a cognitive and/or chronological level;
- the group to which the child belongs, which refers to friends out of school, high-potential groups or class;

The gifted adolescent world 55

- the school, consisting of classroom climate, quality of education, type of teaching, use of technologies and cooperative learning.

Within the microsystem, there is also the family school alliance; in fact, family and school should collaborate in an active way in order to create good schooling. The exosystem, in our model, corresponds to the mass media and the influence this has on the development of ideals and models in the gifted adolescent. The macrosystem, as in the Bronfenbrenner model, is made up of culture.

Family events, important life events, previous school experiences and recognition of high potential are all part of those events mediated by time. As seen in the Bronfenbrenner model, each system affects the other (Bronfenbrenner and Morris, 1998).

Practical suggestions

Isolation

When a gifted child does not have mental-age peers, they may feel socially isolated or experience bullying and exclusion. The socially sensitive gifted child may experience an intense response to perceived rejection, creating a loss of self- and social-confidence.

Introversion vs. extroversion

What might appear as social isolation may be introversion. The gifted child may be satisfied with one or two close friends, be comfortable playing alone or turn to books and pets for companionship.

Gender differences

Studies have shown that at all levels of ability and ages, girls are more advanced in their perceptions of friendship than boys.

Positive connotation

The negative behaviors that adolescents put in place are "bothersome and harmful". Parents and teachers often observe them without knowing what to do. Connoting them positively means "going beyond the manifested"; the adult must try to understand the reasons behind a dysfunctional behavior, so as to be able to help the adolescent with the real difficulty. This is particularly useful for gifted children, when the "cause and effect" of a behavior is not understood.

References

Andover, M. S., Gibb, B. E. (2010). Non-suicidal self-injury, attempted suicide, and suicidal intent among psychiatric inpatients. *Psychiatry Research*, 178, 101–105, doi: 10.1016/j.psychres.2010.03.019.

Asarnow, J. R., Porta, G., Spirito, A. et al. (2011). Suicide attempts and nonsuicidal self-injury in the Treatment of Resistant Depression in Adolescents: Findings from the TORDIA study. *Journal of the American Academy of Child and Adolescent Psychiatry*, 50, 772–781.

Baiocco R., D'Alessio M., Laghi F. (2009). Discrepancies between parents and their children about attitude towards TV advertising. *The Journal of Genetic Psychology*, 170(2), 176–191.

Barton-Breck, A., Heyman, B. (2012). Accentuate the positive, eliminate the negative? The variable value dynamics of non-suicidal self-hurting. *Health, Risk & Society*, 14(5), 445–464.

Baumrind, D. (1966). Effects of authoritative parental control on child behavior. *Child Development*, 37(4), 887–907.

Baumrind, D. (1971). Current patterns of parental authority. *Developmental Psychology Monographs*, 4(1), 1–103.

Baumrind, D. (1991). The influence of parenting style on adolescent competence and substance use. *Journal of Early Adolescence*, 11(1), 56–95.

Belsky, J. (1984). The determinants of parenting: A process model. *Child Development*, 55, 83–96.

Benbow, C. P., Lubinski, D., Shea, D. L., Eftekhari-Sanjani, H. (2000). Sex differences in mathematical reasoning ability: Their status 20 years later. *Psychological Science*, 11, 474–480.

Bigner, J. J. (1994). *Individual and family development: A life-span interdisciplinary approach*. Englewood Cliffs, NJ: Prentice Hall.

Bornstein, M. H. (2002). Parenting infants. In M. H. Bornstein (Ed.), *Handbook of parenting: Volume 1: Children and parenting*. 2nd ed. Mahwah, NJ: Erlbaum, pp. 3–43.

Bronfenbrenner, U. (1979). Contexts of child rearing: Problems and prospects. *American Psychologist*, 34, 844–850.

Bronfenbrenner, U., Morris, P. A. (1998). The ecology of developmental process. In Damon, W., and Lerner, R. M. (Eds.), *Handbook of child psychology, Vol. 1: Theoretical models of human development*. New York: Wiley, pp. 992–1028.

The gifted adolescent world 57

Burks, B.S., Jensen, D. W., Terman, L. M. (1930). *Genetic studies of genius: III. The promise of youth*. Palo Alto, CA: Stanford University Press, p. 508.

Carlson, C., Uppal, S., Prosser, E. C. (2000). Ethnic differences in processes contributing to the self-esteem of early adolescent girls. *Journal of Early Adolescence*, 20, 44–67.

Chapman, A. L., Gratz, K. L., Brown, M. Z. (2006). Solving the puzzle of deliberate self-harm: The experiential avoidance model. *Behavior Research and Therapy*, 44, 371–394.

Charmet, G. P. (2000). *I nuovi adolescenti: padri e madri di fronte a una sfida*. Milan: Raffaello Cortina Editore.

Colangelo, N., Dettmann, D. F. (1983). A review of research on parents and families of gifted children. *Exceptional Children*, 50, 20–27.

Cornell, D., Grossberg, I. (1987). Family environment and personality adjustment in gifted program children. *Gifted Child Quarterly*, 31(2), 59–64.

Cross, T. L. (2007). On the social and emotional lives of gifted children. 2nd ed. Waco, TX: Prufrock Press.

Erikson, E. H. (1968). *Identity: Youth and crisis*. New York: Norton.

Forward, S. (1989). *Toxic parents: Overcoming their hurtful legacy and reclaiming your life*. New York: Bantam Books.

Fox, C., Hawton, K. (2004). *Deliberate self-harm in adolescence*. London: Jessica Kingsley.

Freeman, J. (2010). *Gifted lives: What happens when gifted children grow up*. London: Routledge.

Friedman, R., Rogers, K. (1998). Introduction. In R. Friedman & K. Rogers (Eds.), *Talent in context: Historical and social perspectives on giftedness*. Washington, DC: APA, pp. xv–xxiv.

Golombok, S., Fivush, R. (1994). *Gender development*. New York: Cambridge University Press.

Gualdi, G., Librio, E., Zanetti, M. A. (2016a). When is the challenge for students complicated? Search through high potential and adolescence. *Talincrea. Talento inteligencia y creatividad*, 3(1), 41–59.

Gualdi, G., Zanetti, M. A., Librio, E. (2016b). Italian gifted adolescents: Behaviors, risks and resources. *International Conference ANEIS, Sobredotação: saberes consolidados e desenvolvimentos promissores*, 14–16 May, 19.

Guan, K., Fox, K. R., Prinstein, M. J. (2012). Nonsuicidal self-injury as a time-invariant predictor of adolescent suicide ideation and attempts in a diverse community sample. *Journal of Consulting and Clinical Psychology*, 80(5), 842–849.

Haas, B., Popp, F. (2006). Why do people injure themselves? *Psychopathology*, 39, 10–18.

Hartnett, D. N., Nelson, J. M., Rinn, A. N. (2004). Gifted or ADHD? The possibilities of misdiagnosis. *Roeper Review*, 26(2), 73–76.

Hawton, K., Saunders, K. E. A., O'Connor, R. C. (2012). Self-harm and suicide in adolescents. *Lancet*, 379, 2373–2382.

Hedges, L. V., Nowell, A. (1995). Sex differences in mental test scores, variability, and numbers of high-scoring individuals. *Science*, 269(5220), 41–45.

Heller, K. A. (Ed.). (2000). *Begabungsdiagnostik* (2nd ed.) [Assessment of giftedness]. Bern: Huber Publishing.

Hooley, J. M., St Germain, S. A. (2013). Nonsuicidal self-injury, pain, and self-criticism: Does changing self-worth change pain endurance in people who engage in self-injury? *Clinical Psychological Science*, 2(3), 297–305.

Jolly, J. L., Matthews, M. S. (2012). A critique of the literature on parenting gifted learners. *Journal for the Education of the Gifted*, 35, 259–290.

Karnes, M. B., Shwedel, A. M. (1987). Differences in attitudes and practices between fathers of young gifted and fathers of young non-gifted children: A pilot study. *Gifted Child Quarterly*, 31(2), 79–82.

Klonsky, E. D., Muehlenkamp, J. J. (2007). Self-injury: A research review for the practitioner. *Journal of Clinical Psychology*, 63, 1045–1056.

Kulieke, M. J., Olszewski-Kubilius, P. (1989). The influence of family values and climate on the development of talent. In J. VanTassel-Baska & P. Olszewski-Kubilius (Eds.), *Patterns of influence on gifted learners*. New York, NY: Teachers College Press, pp. 40–59.

Moon, S. M., Reis, S. M. (2004). Acceleration and twice exceptional students. In Colangelo, N., Assouline, S. G., Gross, M. U. M. (Eds.). *A nation deceived: How schools hold back America's brightest students* (Volume 2). Iowa City, IA: The Connie Belin & Jacqueline N Blank Center for Gifted Education and Talent Development, pp. 109–119.

Moon, S. M., Jurich, J. A., Feldhusen, J. F. (1996). Families of gifted children: Cradles of development. In R. C. Friedman & K. B. Rogers (Eds.), *Talent in context: Historical and social perspectives on giftedness*. Washington, DC: APA, pp. 81–99.

Morawska, A., Sanders, M. R. 2009. An evaluation of a behavioural parenting intervention for parents of gifted children. *Behaviour Research and Therapy*, 47, 463–470.

Muehlenkamp, J. J. (2005). Self-injurious behavior as a separate clinical syndrome. *American Journal of Orthopsychiatry*, 75, 324–333.

Muehlenkamp, J. J., Claes, L., Havertape, L., Plener, P. (2012). International prevalence of adolescent nonsuicidal self-injury and deliberate self-harm. *Child and Adolescent Psychiatry and Mental Health*, 6, 10–18.

Neihart, M., Reis, S. M., Robinson, N. M., Moon, S. M. (Eds.) (2002). *The social and emotional development of gifted children: What do we know?* Waco, TX: Prufrock Press.

Nock, M. K., Wedig, M. M., Janis, I. B., Deliberto, T. L. (2008). Self-injurious thoughts and behaviours. In J. Hunsley, E. J. Mash (Eds.),

The gifted adolescent world 59

Guide to assessments that work. New York: Oxford Univ. Press, pp. 158–179.

Olszewski, P., Kulieke, M. J., Buescher, T. (1987). The influence of the family environment on the development of talent: A literature review. *Journal for the Education of the Gifted*, 11, 6–28.

Pfeiffer S. I., Stocking V. B. (2000). Vulnerabilities of academically gifted students. *Special Services in the Schools*, 16, 83–93.

Reis, S. M. (2002). Gifted females in elementary and secondary school. In Neihart, M., Reis, S. M., Robinson, N. M., Moon, S. M. (Eds.), *The social and emotional development of gifted children: What do we know?* Waco, TX: Prufrock Press, pp. 125–136.

Reis, S. M., Hebert, T. P., Diaz, E. I., Maxfield, L. R., Ratley, M. E. (1995). *Case studies of talented students who achieve and underachieve in an urban high school* (Research Monograph No. 95120). Storrs, CT: National Research Center on the Gifted and Talented, University of Connecticut.

Reitman, D., Rhode, P. C., Hupp, S. D., Altobello, C. (2002). Development and validity of the Parental Authority Questionnaire – Revised. *Journal of Psychopathology and Behavioral Assessment*, 24, 119–127.

Rossi Monti, M., D'Agostino, A. (2009). *Autolesionismo*. Roma: Carocci.

Ricci, A. (2011). *Famiglia tra risorse ed emergenza. Un percorso educativo*. Elledici, Torino.

Ricci, C. (2008). *Hikikomori: adolescenti in volontaria reclusione*. Milano: FrancoAngeli.

Rinn, A. N., Reynolds, M. J. (2012). Overexcitabilities and ADHD in the gifted: An examination. *Roeper Review*, 34, 38–45. doi:10.1080/02783193.2012.627551.

Saito, T. (1998). *Shakaiteki Hikikomori: Owaranai Shishunki (Social withdrawal: Unfinished puberty)*. Tokyo: PHP-Kenkyujo.

Silverman, L. K. (1998). Perfectionism. *Gifted Education International*, 13(3), 216–255.

Sword, L. (2001). *Psycho-social needs: Understanding the emotional, intellectual and social uniqueness of growing up gifted*. Gifted & Creative Services Australia Pty Ltd. Retrieved from http://talentdevelop.com/articles/PsychosocNeeds.html.

VanTassel-Baska, J. (2003). Introduction to curriculum for gifted and talented students: A 25-year retrospective and prospective. Thousand Oaks, CA: Corwin Press.

Wenar, C. (1994). *Developmental psychopathology: From infancy through adolescence*. New York: McGraw-Hill.

Whitfield, C. L. (1987). *Healing the child within: Discovery and recovery for adult children of dysfunctional families*. Deerfield Beach, FL: Health Communications.

Wilkinson, P., Goodyer, I. (2011). Non-suicidal self-injury. *European Child & Adolescent Psychiatry, 20,* 103–108.

Zanetti, M. A. (2017). *Bambini e ragazzi ad alto potenziale. Una guida per educatori e famiglie.* Roma: Carocci.

Zanetti, M. A., Gualdi, G., Librio, E. (2016). *Adolescenti ad alto potenziale cognitivo: rischi e risorse.* Poster XXIX Congresso Nazionale AIP, Sezione di Psicologia dello Sviluppo e dell'Educazione, Vicenza (8–10 settembre).

Zielenziger, M. (2008). *Non voglio più vivere alla luce del sole.* Roma: Elliot.

Chapter 3

Learning for gifted students is not so easy

Maria Assunta Zanetti

Introduction

Research has shown that there are neurological differences both in development and cerebral functioning between average and gifted people.[1] It has been possible to show that intelligence is related to the dynamic properties of cortical maturation.[2] In particular, studies show how in gifted people, the prefrontal cortex follows atypical development, with delayed structural and metabolic maturation: in the early stages of life, it appears thinner than the average population.

Research also suggests that gifted people favor the right hemisphere, which seems to be more developed than average.[3] It has been observed that the interhemispheric transmission of information is faster, regardless of the nature of the stimulus or the hemisphere usually involved in carrying out a specific task;[4] indeed, white matter (composed of axons and coated with myelin) allows greater connectivity between hemispheres.[5]

These characteristics can sometimes represent a weakness. Discrepancy between reasoning abilities and cognitive dimensions has been observed, compromising the correct use of executive functions and metacognition, which are important factors for academic success.

The executive functions are nothing more than the cognitive abilities necessary to plan, implement and successfully carry out a behavior aimed at a purpose. They include cognitive and self-regulating processes that allow the monitoring and control of thoughts and actions, such as inhibition, planning, attentional flexibility, and the identification and correction of errors. We can see a different

The role of executive functions at school

As we have already seen in the previous chapters, giftedness is characterized by an asynchronous development, not only for the gap between accelerated cognitive development and emotional development aligned with age but also for some aspects related to cognitive functioning.

The condition of gifted students at school is often difficult because of the malfunctioning of executive functions with the risk of seeing compromised learning and academic success.

Having a high IQ is no guarantee of academic success. Often pupils with IQ scores of 136 fail to complete an activity or forget to continue an activity that they have started; in practice, knowing what to do and when to do it is directed by the executive functions (EF).

Not all gifted students struggle with executive functioning, but gifted children are often more likely to encounter these struggles than other students. Some gifted students may have very fast processing speed, without having to develop their basic skills. Other gifted children's processing speed shows a great lag behind their other cognitive processes. These children may struggle to show task initiation skills that would then look like a lack of motivation.

When it comes to developing executive functioning skills, though, there really is a downside to school being "too easy." If you are easily able to understand your lessons, memorize the key details and recall them later, there is no need to develop a set of study skills. Until middle school these students often do not experience failure even without studying. This leads to their brains not having learnt to study. Entry to high school is often disastrous and this phenomenon is not limited to studying. In fact, if during elementary school they leaned on their great memory, they did not have the opportunity to learn and practice assignment management. They have difficulty finding priorities, often memorizing details but not retaining them. Having a talent for information can actually hamper the development of these output skills.

Executive functioning must be present throughout a person's development and therefore it cannot be satisfied when a child learns easily. That means that everyone should be in the condition of being adequately challenged. "Too easy" is a problem

Learning for gifted students 63

that should not be taken lightly. Children who are not challenged enough miss out on an opportunity to practice critical executive functioning skills. They are more likely to become risk-averse and not tackle challenges that are outside their comfort zones. When you are challenged with work that pushes your intellectual limits (without putting yourself in a state of frustration), a lot of development can happen – in terms of both input and output. The EF are a set of mental processes that help us connect past experiences with present action. We use these learned skills to make plans, set goals, keep track of time, complete tasks and much more. The EF are at the base of some skills:

1 Attention (obtaining and maintaining)
2 Inhibition and impulse control
3 Initiation and persistence
4 Goal setting and prioritizing
5 Planning and organization
6 Time management
7 Flexible thinking
8 Self-regulation and monitoring
9 Working memory

The simultaneous possession of these skills favors the correct processing of information and guarantees successful learning. When one or more are not used correctly, learning can fail.

It is not uncommon to find a gifted child who has very high cognitive abilities yet struggles with one or more aspects of executive functioning. Executive functioning involves self-regulating attention, mood and behavior, in order to get complex tasks done well (Table 3.1).

The EF govern the central lobe and develop in earliest infancy and continue throughout childhood and adolescence. Often gifted students have to learn to use them consciously. Furthermore, research indicates that success and happiness in life are not achieved just through intelligence, but also through an ability to apply oneself to chosen tasks and work through the process. EF skills tend to transfer across domains; if a child learns how to self-regulate in learning one kind of task, it will be easier to learn to self-regulate in other areas. As adults, we can also help children develop their own EF skills (Schnack et al., 2015).

Table 3.1 Executive functioning in gifted learners

They understand everything in class and do not develop study skills
They can memorize homework and never learn to actually write it down
They complete homework in 15 minutes and never have to manage their time
They innately understand material in class and do not learn to take notes
They have never struggled in school and do not know how to overcome obstacles
Assignments are intuitive for them, so there is never a need for planning larger projects

Gifted students who have a higher IQ in their primary school years seem to have an extended period in adolescence during which they retain the ability to learn at a rapid pace, just like much younger children. The later maturation of the cortex may explain why gifted students tend to lag behind in EF skills compared to the typical development time; but most do catch up eventually (Figure 3.1).

These students need more scaffolding and support for EF in middle school, when they may be expected to have already mastered these skills.

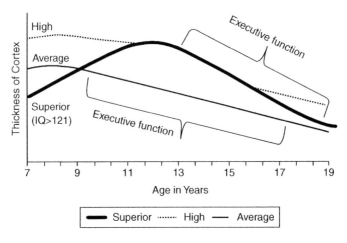

Figure 3.1 Changes in the thickness of the brain's cortex between the ages in subjects with superior, high and average intelligence.

Weaknesses in EF tend to affect all areas of children's lives, including some of what seem like basic self-regulation or home life tasks, and can be extremely frustrating for parents and siblings. In general, when something is chronically frustrating to family members, it is because children want to do too many things at the same time and they do not know how to start.

We cannot trace the difficulties in the conscious use of EF to a single cause; however, it is possible to identify a list of behaviors that can compromise optimal functioning:

- inhibition of impulses – stopping to choose an appropriate response
- previewing likely consequences of action (both short- and long-term)
- holding and manipulating information in working memory
- sustaining attention despite distraction or fatigue
- planning, both short- and long-term
- saliency determination – figuring out which details are important
- task initiation – getting started on a chosen task
- depth of processing – choosing a level that is not too superficial or too consuming
- time control – maintaining an appropriate speed and rhythm for work
- development of automaticity – making a skill routine so it takes no conscious effort
- satisfaction – perceiving and deriving pleasure from reinforcers
- organization – both internal (thoughts) and external (materials)
- time management – predicting how long things will take, planning and acting
- flexibility – adapting strategies or plans to respond to mistakes or new information
- self-monitoring – observing one's own performance and comparing it to standards
- emotional self-regulation – being aware of and managing feelings
- metacognition – being aware of one's own thought processes

Developmental executive functions

To foster learning and the healthy functioning of a gifted child, it is necessary that teachers provide cues, reminders and a way to determine whether or not a task has been completed. The child can then get used to the system rather than just be reminded to do the task. As they demonstrate the ability to perform more independently, the level of support can be gradually phased out, and new goals can be established.

Many parents complain about the feeling of being the child's substitute front lobe, and despair about being able to get them to take over. They impose a fix-it-all-now executive system themselves, and the harder they try to enforce compliance, the harder it will be to meet the needs of their child. Therefore, they conclude that the child is incapable of change.

All too often, children figure out at some level that they are fundamentally incompetent and cannot achieve anything important. These are two serious motivation-killers. They also often figure out that learning to self-regulate is the parents' goal, not their own, and become resistant – almost all people tend to resist what they view as being imposed upon them.

Children often have a hard time maintaining a focus on the long-term goal of their own growth and development. Their weaknesses in EF and motivation often lead them to adopt short-term goals that serve to make their lives easier (get people to ask less of them, get mom to leave them alone, get something they haven't earned, get the work finished with minimal effort, etc.). These strategies tend to be harmful in the long-term, often seriously interfering with their learning. It is important to be aware of these strategies and to not allow them to work and toil.

It is important to help the child learn to use these skills to allow them to experience academic success and avoid frustration and situations of social isolation.

Every EF skill can be broken down, taught, practiced and mastered. The key is to learn these skills before they are critically needed for success in a tough class.

Even if you think that a gifted child does not really need to write everything down or study, especially at the beginning of the school path, it is advisable for the teacher or tutor to help them develop these skills to guarantee them a peaceful future at school. Indeed, every child should learn to organize school materials, track and prioritize assignments, take notes from a textbook, study effectively, and write responses and paragraphs with structure. These skills are just as important as learning to solve equations or complex reasoning.

Some educators are now recommending teaching children EF skills and processes systematically starting in the elementary grades. One reason is that even in early elementary, teachers are requiring students to complete long-term projects, as well as lengthy reading and writing ones.

It is critical that every child is taught these kinds of strategies. They impact on students in a way that will allow them to increase their level of competence. Even second-grade students are expected to coordinate multiple sub-skills.

We must keep in mind that EF strategies are not a "one size fits all." They must understand their own learning profile and strengths and weaknesses as well as which strategies work for them.

Dealing with EF can lead children to experience a variety of problems in their friendships, peer relationships and other social interactions. Every day, behaviors like sharing, taking turns, picking up subtle social cues and staying attentive in class can be very difficult for children who struggle with EF skills.

Perhaps most importantly, teachers and parents must continue to provide encouragement and support, but above all recognize the effort made.

Practical suggestions

How can I help a child make the most of executive functions?

Attention: make sure the child is focused on the task and challenge it by proposing tasks that activate it, then start from their interests for in-depth learning. The goal is to have sustained attention in spite of fatigue, distractibility and boredom. However, there are a number of distractions to focused attention. See if you can identify those distractions that interfere with your child's attention.

Inhibition and impulse control: this is the ability to stop and think before acting. Promote moments of reflection through verbal exchanges and use of diaries and focus on the accuracy of results. Sometimes children behave impulsively because they do not listen to the directions. Pay attention to how deliveries are presented to avoid misunderstandings and help them know how to justify their thinking by helping them learn to think before they act.

Lack of frustration tolerance can be a big factor in impulse control. Teach them how to manage anger so they can calm down when they are upset. Time out can be a great way for children to learn how to calm themselves down, as long as it is used as a consequence and not as a punishment.

Initiation and persistence: initiation is the ability to recognize when it is time to begin a task without procrastinating. Children lacking in this skill have trouble starting homework or put off projects until the last minute. They are sometimes seen as lazy or unmotivated. Often their inaction is due to their perfectionism, therefore they do not feel able to realize what they have thought or are overwhelmed by all they have to do.

- Persistence is relative to the task; therefore, we must propose activities that they consider meaningful.
- Help children identify successful strategies for problem-solving.
- Offer praise that is specific and meaningful to what has actually been done; however, avoid vague words and exaggerated praise.

Goal setting and prioritizing: categorizing activities is an important part of the prioritization process, as it provides a foundation on which students can build their schedules. Once tasks have been grouped according to importance, students can rely on their knowledge of time and task to allot the appropriate amount of time for each activity. Compulsory tasks (e.g., homework, jobs, enrichment activities) should be accomplished first, followed by aspirational tasks (e.g., activities that are enjoyable, interesting).

The goals are:

- realistic
- begin with the end in mind (backwards planning)
- prioritize long- and short-term tasks (day-to-day)
- select most important information in notes
- with fixed deadlines (intrinsically set or imposed)

Planning and organization: this concerns the ability to create steps to reach a goal. Gifted children often have difficulty

Learning for gifted students   69

planning and setting priorities. They have trouble thinking through the steps required to achieve a goal. They tend to underestimate a project's complexity and time requirements. They need to develop these skills for homework, studying, writing and especially for completing long-term projects.

Time management: for gifted children it is important to learn how to manage time; they are often immersed in their thoughts and ideas and lose track of time.

It is important that parents and teachers provide tools to manage their time (diaries, schemes, familiar routines, calendar, planning).

Flexible thinking: this is the ability to change strategies or revise plans when conditions change. Children who behave in ways that are inflexible have trouble when a familiar routine is disrupted, or a task becomes complicated. They get frustrated when a first attempt to solve a problem is not successful. They are unable to see new ways to do familiar tasks or to make another choice when the first choice proves unworkable.

Flexible thinking is so important for academic performance because it allows transition time when switching between rest and work to help a person cope with unexpected changes to routines, schedules, homework and projects.

Self-regulation and monitoring: this is the ability to monitor and evaluate your own performance. Children who are weak at monitoring may not be aware that they are not following directions until someone points this out. They tend to misjudge their efforts and have trouble adjusting what they are doing based on feedback or cues. They are often completely surprised by a low grade on a test or project.

Working memory: this is the ability to hold information in your mind and use it to complete a task. Working memory usually occurs in two forms. Verbal (auditory) working memory taps into our sound (hearing) system. Visual-spatial working memory is a kind of visual sketchpad. We envision something in our mind's eye. We use both when following multi-step directions. Help students organize the material:

- create checklists with pictures for younger children
- focus on a single goal or task to complete. Multitasking is not always effective!

70 Maria Assunta Zanetti

Some strategies:

- choose a single skill and develop specific strategies to improve that skill; proceed gradually
- raise the awareness of the young person about executive deficit functions
- procrastination is not necessarily laziness or lack of interest
- disorganization and disorder are not always symptoms of incapacity or stupidity
- find a balance between the mental dimension and procedural aspects
- make use of their high intellectual abilities to develop plans

It is indeed important to support the development of these skills and processes involved in EF from primary school.

To facilitate the functioning of the EF, the learning proposed at school should go from being focused on content (or what to know) to how to do or learn things, and on proposing metacognitive strategies that teach students to think about how they think and learn. It is critical that every child is taught these kinds of strategies.

Perhaps most importantly, teachers and parents must continue to provide consistent and ongoing encouragement and support. Children with social challenges may also have low self-esteem. Recognize even the smallest improvement in the student. Knowing that you care about their progress can be very reassuring.

Notes

1 Geake, 2007; Mrazik and Dombrowski, 2010.
2 Shaw et al., 2006.
3 Desco et al., 2011; Winner, 2000.
4 Singh and O'Boyle, 2004.
5 Tetreault et al., 2016; Virdis et al., 2016.
6 Satre-Riba and Viana, 2016.

References

Desco, M., Navas-Sanchez, F. J., Sanchez-González, J., Reig, S., Robles, O., Franco, C., Arango, C. (2011). Mathematically gifted adolescents use more extensive and more bilateral areas of the fronto-parietal network than controls during executive functioning and fluid reasoning tasks. *Neuroimage*, 57 (1), 281–292.

Geake, J. G. (2007). *The Neurobiology of Giftedness*. Westminster Institute of Education, Oxford Brookes University, UK.

Mrazik, M., Dombrowski, S. C. (2010). The neurobiological foundations of giftedness. *Roeper Review*, 32, 224–234.

Satre-Riba, S., Viana, L. (2016). High intellectual ability: Cognitive management and talent expression. *Revista de neurologia*, 62 (s01), S65–S71.

Schnack, H. G., van Haren, N. E., Brouwer, R. M., Evans, A., Durston, S., Boomsma, D. I., Kahn, R. S., Hulshoff Po, H. E. (2015). Changes in thickness and surface area of the human cortex and their relationship with intelligence. *Cereb Cortex*, 25 (6), 1608–1617.

Shaw, P., Greenstein, D., Lerch, J., Clasen, L., Lenroot, R., Gogtay, N., Evans, A., Rapoport, J., Giedd, J. (2006). Intellectual ability and cortical development in children and adolescent. *Nature*, 440, 676–679.

Singh, H., O'Boyle, M. W. (2004). Interhemispheric interaction during global–local processing in mathematically gifted adolescents, average-ability youth, and college students. *Neuropsychology*, 18 (2), 371–377.

Tetreault, N., Haase, J., Duncan, S. (2016). *The Gifted Brain*. Gifted Research and Outreach, Inc, 1–25.

Virdis, D., Neri, I., Oliva, G., Riccioni, A., Terribili, M. (2016). Il bambino gifted: Aspetti neuropsicologici e riabilitativi. *Disturbi di Attenzione e Iperattività*, 12 (1), 29–44.

Winner, E. (2000). The origins and ends of giftedness. *American Psychologist*, 55 (1), 159–169.

Chapter 4

Educating gifted and talented students in everyday school practice

Michael Cascianelli

Introduction

For more than a century, researchers have sought to describe, identify and support gifted students. Seminal theories and empirical work have built on earlier research, integrating or often dissenting over conceptions in this field of study.[1] As a result, numerous scholars have been debating conceptions of giftedness whilst incorporating related ideas such as "above-average ability",[2] "high ability"[3] and "cognitive analytic abilities".[4] Therefore, such discussion has led to confusion for teachers, practitioners and schools aiming to address the needs of their gifted pupils.

A major concern in the field of gifted education is that the regular classroom environment provides little challenge for those students who have already mastered the content or have the potential to learn new material at an above-average pace.[5] This is supported by evidence gathered from research studies that have investigated instructional differentiation across subject areas in both primary and secondary schools.[6] Differentiated instruction has been described as the act of shaping content, process and product based on the individual needs of each learner. It is an educational strategy that aims to respond to the different needs of different students. Stepanek (1999) defines differentiated instruction as "a continuous process of learning about students' needs and interests and using that knowledge to guide instruction" (p. 18). However, Brighton, Hertberg, Moon, Tomlinson and Callahan (2005) found that, when teachers do differentiate instruction in their classrooms, the focus is largely on students with learning difficulties, which suggests that gifted students do not need differentiation. Nonetheless, gifted children, like all students, need a curriculum that challenges them and that best meets their educational needs.[7] However, Hertberg-Davis (2009) and Plucker (2015) argue that the current practice of differentiation can disconcert the needs of the gifted and the talented. What then serves as a good pragmatic basis to allow teachers to structure lesson plans for the provision of gifted and talented students? This chapter aims to provide teachers, schools' administrators and parents with an outline of services reviewed from the academic literature to be implemented in schools to allow gifted and talented students to express their full potential.

Enrichment and gifted programs

It is argued that schools and teachers may need to review the ways in which learning for gifted and talented students occurs whilst investing in the depth and breadth of the services provided for these students. Enrichment refers to experiences, activities and programming options to supplement the regular school curriculum. Taber and Riga (2006) argue that enrichment has to be different in kind from the regular lessons experienced by students. Therefore, enrichment may involve topics to be covered in depth by gifted students who will then explore broader issues related to a specific subject. This suggests that enrichment activities should be thoroughly planned for gifted children, especially since students remain in their own classroom context.

Renzulli's Schoolwide Enrichment Model (SEM) is a school organizational system that aims to develop creative productivity by allowing students to experience a variety of challenging activities based on their abilities, interests and learning styles. Significantly, the importance of Renzulli's conception of giftedness is the basis of his Enrichment Triad Model (1977), which involves three types of enriched instruction to support gifted children. As Reis and Renzulli (2003, 2009) suggest, Type I enrichment activities involve stimulating new interests in gifted children, through exploratory activities. Type II activities include critical and creative thinking and learning-to-learn skills through group activities. Type III enrichment aims to develop higher-level research and creative abilities through small-group or individual analysis of real problems. This system employs a rigorous set of strategies such as the Total Talent portfolio, enrichment clusters and curriculum

74 Michael Cascianelli

compacting to support all students in achieving their potential (Renzulli & Reis, 1997, 2014).

There have been a number of research studies evaluating the impact of this model on both gifted and non-gifted children. These studies have found that the model, or models derived from SEM, have a positive impact especially in relation to student creativity and productivity (Delcourt, 1993; Hébert, 1993). In his article Houghton (2014) aimed to capture the voice of 16 gifted students from school years 8 to 11 who had participated in an enrichment cluster in their first two years of primary school. The students involved in the study represented a wide range of backgrounds and five of them had been identified as being on the autistic spectrum. The case study was carried out during the Easter holidays of 2010 at Rawmarsh City Learning Centre in the United Kingdom, where the enrichment cluster aimed to address the lack of provision for gifted students. OWLETS, as the enrichment cluster was named, was designed on the basis of Renzulli's SEM. Houghton aimed to investigate the students' perspectives on their experiences of OWLETS and the impact of these experiences on their subsequent education. On the one hand, findings related to the five students on the autistic spectrum suggest that they had had positive experiences during their primary education and struggles in secondary education. On the other hand, the other 11 students preferred their secondary education to their primary education. However, the study does not offer an explicit discussion on the depth of information described by the 16 students. Such a consideration would have been important to acknowledge since the students were asked to report something they had experienced a long time before the data collection of this study.

Moreover, all students viewed experiences relating to personalized learning and effective relationship between teacher and student as key. In support of these positive findings, Houghton's qualitative study clearly presents the methods used in the research process such as pupils' scripts and videos. Furthermore, the author acknowledges the choices involved in the adoption of phenomenological methodology for the study as well as providing examples of qualitative data analysis to show how themes emerged. Although information related to the research paradigm adopted by the researcher is missing, data analysis shown with the inclusion of transcripts within the article might perhaps suggest Houghton's interpretivist stance. Finally, the findings shown

Educating gifted and talented students 75

within this qualitative case study indicate that Renzulli's model, in this simple structure, has the potential to enrich the school and the lives of all students, including the exceptionally talented ones. Despite the recent and positive experience shown in the latter study, there seems to be a lack of investigation in the literature in relation to what pupils think about the SEM, what positive outcomes there may be and what challenges teachers may face. Moreover, there seems to be a gap in the literature in relation to what arises from interviews or observations of the daily implementation of the models or even what might be revealed by an investigation that looks at the transferability of this model in other school contexts. This is a reason why Subotnik, Olszewski-Kubilius and Worrell (2011) argue that, although enrichment is considered to be a frequent programming option for gifted students, there is still a lack of formal evaluation of these programs.

Whilst Renzulli's SEM focuses on providing the same enriched education to all students in the classroom whether they are gifted and talented or not, gifted programs may have an organization of services whereby gifted students might be in different courses compared to non-gifted students. A few studies have analyzed students' perceptions on their gifted programs implemented within schools. For instance, highly gifted primary school students indicated numerous advantages of their gifted programs involving increased choices and learning, greater challenge and less dependence on textbooks (Moon, Swift & Shallenberger, 2002). Similarly, middle-school students reported that their programs allowed them to have better teaching staff and curricula and that they received more academic opportunities and experiences (Berlin, 2009). In the same work, however, the same students expressed that they had to deal with harder homework and high amounts of work, together with higher expectations of teachers.

Whilst some studies have focused on the academic experiences of gifted students within enrichment programs, other studies have analyzed how these programs supported gifted students' social and emotional functioning. Gifted students in their primary school found that meeting new gifted students and making new friends were social advantages of their program (Moon, Callahan, et al., 2002). Likewise, high-school gifted students expressed that their program provided them with social recognition, opportunities to meet other intellectual peers and increased self-confidence (Kerr, Colangelo & Gaeth, 1988).

Students also identified emotional advantages as distinct from social advantages. One advantage involved the perception of gifted students being accepted by their gifted peers (Moon, Callahan, et al., 2002). A second advantage was found in a sense of belonging whereby students in the same gifted program did not feel like outsiders (Moon, Callahan, et al., 2002). In relation to emotional functioning, gifted students who identified positive emotional outcomes were inclined to describe positive outcomes also in academic achievement. In particular, positive emotions led to greater challenge and improved learning experiences in the gifted program.

On the other hand, students also expressed social and emotional disadvantages. For instance, elementary students described losing friends from a general education program or being mocked by students outside of the gifted class (Moon, Callahan, et al., 2002). This is followed by students perceiving increased competition in relation to being with other gifted students who were more intelligent (Marsh, Plucker & Stocking, 2001). For example, some students expressed that they were not confident about themselves when considering that there were more students at their same level. Although being with other gifted peers represented intellectual and social advantages for some students, others may feel uncomfortable intellectually, socially and emotionally because of self-reflection in relation to peers (Kitsantas, Bland & Chirinos, 2017). Other studies have analyzed emotional disadvantages. For instance, middle-school students described great pressure from parental expectation and reported that some of their teachers viewed their being gifted negatively. Therefore, this led them to put more pressure on these students to perform better than their peers (Berlin, 2009). Moreover, some studies have investigated bullying as an emotional disadvantage for gifted students (Feldman et al., 2014). In a study conducted by Peterson and Ray (2006), the researchers analyzed the experiences of bullying of 432 gifted eighth-grade students from 11 states. These students were asked about experiences of physical and nonphysical bullying dating back to their kindergarten year. Bullying was identified by 67% of the students at one point during their K-8 years, with male students reporting a higher prevalence (73%) than female students (63%). The most recurrent forms of bullying as reported by the gifted students were teasing, name-calling and being derided by other students who were not in the same program.

Overall, empirical research has identified that although gifted students face various forms of issues within their school years (Feldhusen & Moon, 1992), they indeed benefit by participating in gifted programs. Therefore, exploring students' perceptions and experiences in gifted programs is fundamental in understanding how to best foster their well-being in schools (Coleman, Micko & Cross, 2015). Enrichment and gifted programs involve services that provide students and teachers with a set of possibilities to use in the classroom, such as independent work, subject and/or grade-based acceleration and different forms of students' grouping. However, before going into exploring what the academic literature has to offer in relation to these services, enrichment and gifted programs are also systems where gifted and talented students can experience daily challenges in their specific areas of talent.

Challenging gifted and talented students

In Bloom's (1985) longitudinal study, gifted children were provided with a continuous progression of more and more difficult expectations which were determined by themselves together with a tutor, teacher or mentor. The students could reflect on their progress as they advanced in the knowledge and skills required in their talent areas and then developed their "benchmark of progress". In studying gifted teenagers, Csikszentmihalyi, Rathunde and Whalen (1993) found that when these students were not given the possibility to advance in their area of talent, there was an increase in psychological distress, stress and boredom. Although the same researchers suggest the need for talented students to persevere in any talent area, often independently, it is argued that greater development rises when both school and home contexts provide opportunities for talent development through challenge. This greater development is often analyzed as an estimate of yearly growth that is possible to observe when a student participates in talent development activities through a school program within a specific area of talent. The expectation of yearly growth using Bloom's (1985) estimate, for instance, is close to 3 years of growth in the talent area per year. Moreover, it is also argued that the yearly growth will vary based on the intensity of the daily challenge and mentoring provided to the students. Kulik and Kulik (1992) showed that for equally gifted students not provided with daily challenge, their progress will be 1 year's growth for attending school for a year, while a "challenged" student's progress will be equivalent to 1 year ahead in 2 years, 3 years ahead in 4 years and so forth (Rogers, 2007). Although daily challenge is reported to be important for talent development, research suggests that consistent, even if not daily, challenge is significant to gifted students outside of their area of talent. Therefore, this supports the idea that every identified gifted student must be provided with a consistent and progressively more challenging curriculum structured across grades, whilst building levels of skills in and out of areas of talent (Tomlinson et al., 2002; Tyler-Wood, Mortenson, Putney & Cass, 2000).

The significance of the latter consideration is that it opens the discourse on how to better structure challenging curricula in support of the consistent growth of gifted students. The implication of this may be in structuring independent learning, regrouping students by ability level or implementing subject/grade acceleration. Archambault et al. (1993) support the idea of finding a school organization of services outside of the regular classroom. Moreover, the researchers argue that if left to the regular classroom teacher to implement, teaching problems will occur in relation to other responsibilities such as the lack of training and lack of motivation to differentiate in a progressively challenging manner. The pull-out program can be flexible to structure activities to gather gifted students together for a significant portion of the school week. For this to be effective, however, Vaughn, Feldhusen and Asher (1991) argue that the pull-out needs to be on extensions of the regular curriculum offered or on specific skills within a curriculum area.

The next three sections of this chapter will serve as a guideline to investigate three main services involved within enrichment and gifted programs.

Gifted and talented students need to work independently on their interest and talent areas

In a review of research on gifted learning styles, Rogers (2002) found that when compared to regular students, gifted students are more likely to prefer working independently on projects and self-instructional material. However, the effects of independent

Educating gifted and talented students 79

learning on gifted students seem to be diversified. In primary school years, for instance, where no improvement in overall achievement is detected, growth is identified in self-reliance, ability to identify a topic focus, and a rise in critical and creative thinking (Pentelbury, 2000). On the other hand, in secondary school years, Callahan and Smith (1990) reported a general increase in achievement and improved motivation. From these considerations, it is questionable that being gifted or wanting to carry independent study does not guarantee that one will be effective in an independent learning activity (Rogers, 2007). The literature in this field reports a number of curriculum development systems for organizing independent study services within a school. These are Betts's (1986) autonomous learning model, Treffinger's (1986) self-directed learning model and Renzulli and Reis's (2014) Type III activities within SEM.

Specifically, one of Renzulli's enrichment activities focuses on gifted students working independently to foster investigation of real problems. This means that schools and teachers are to organize ways to best meet the needs of those gifted students who may have an inclination into a specific area of interest or talent. However, it is argued that determining a gifted student's area of interest or talent is not always as straightforward as it may seem. The Total Talent (TT) portfolio is a tool that serves to bring together all the information of a specific student in relation to strengths, interests, talents and learning styles (Renzulli & Reis, 2014).

Overall, Nasca and Davis (1981) report that independent study does have an impact on motivation to learn new material and there is potential to structure it through the use of a curriculum model such as the previously mentioned Renzulli's SEM and well-trained teachers. By allowing students to foster independent learning, schools and teachers will face a situation where gifted students will master what is about to be offered well in advance compared to other students. This consideration leads schools to find ways to structure these students' individualized learning in a way to give them credit for their achievements. Such credit is found in curriculum compacting as a system to assess the implementation of a differentiated activity when students demonstrate mastery in one or more areas of talent. The academic impact of curriculum compacting is found to be powerful, especially in relation to mathematics and sciences (up to four

80 Michael Cascianelli

fifths of a year's academic achievement), when activities have been progressively advanced in complexity. One of the most relevant studies on curriculum compacting was carried out by Reis, Westberg, Kulikowich and Purcell (1998) in the United States on 27 geographically different school districts. The researchers found that when 36% to 54% of either reading or mathematics curricula were removed or replaced by differentiated activities, gifted students achieved as well as other gifted peers whose curriculum had not been compacted. In summary, individualized learning, as well as curriculum compacting, has the potential to give gifted students the chance to be challenged and to feel that they are making progress. All issues, on the other hand, occur when gifted students need to repeat what they have already mastered and therefore lapse into underachievement (Colangelo & Assouline, 1995) and to lowered academic self-esteem (Hoekman, McCormick & Gross, 1999).

Academic acceleration as an effective intervention for gifted students

Acceleration is an umbrella term that involves the school services necessary to meet the needs of gifted and talented students through advanced course placement, educational curriculum, experiences and opportunities. Acceleration is also both a curriculum model that students may receive as they progress at a faster pace through a school curriculum and a service delivery model in students receiving it at a younger age compared to their peers. It is argued that academic acceleration, in one or more of its 20 forms, is the most effective model for supporting the needs of gifted and talented students through the conventional school curriculum (Finn & Wright, 2015; Rogers, 2015). Acceleration is mainly divided into subject-based and grade-based acceleration and its primary feature is that in accelerating both the pace and content of a regular school curriculum, this process shortens the number of years that a student spends in the school system.

Subject-based acceleration involves providing students with an advanced level of content, skills and understanding compared to a typical age or grade level in a specific subject (Rogers, 2015). Typically, subject-based acceleration allows students to remain within their age group for most of the school day and yet students have the opportunity to learn content at a higher grade level. For instance, a student enrolled in a grade 5 class performing above the average level in mathematics compared to their peers may be enrolled in a grade 7 class to advance their own skills. There are various types of subject-based acceleration such as single-subject acceleration, dual enrolment, credit-by-examination or even curriculum compacting. These types of acceleration can be implemented with individual students/and or groups of students. The latter form of acceleration, for instance, could relate to enrichment clusters within Renzulli and Reis's (2014) SEM.

Grade-based acceleration, on the other hand, involves shortening the number of years that a student spends in a school system (Rogers, 2015). This strategy is commonly known as grade skipping as students may skip grades through their education. Grade-based acceleration includes early entrance to school such as entering in 1st grade as opposed to kindergarten, grade telescoping and early entrance to college/university. Regarding early entrance to kindergarten, Robinson (2004) suggests that candidates would be not more than three months younger from the cut-off birth date designated by a school. These candidates would also undergo psychological evaluation and academic assessment on readiness and emotional regulation. This is because the performance of young students on academic achievement is more variable than that of older students. In order to make such decisions, the Iowa Acceleration Scale (Assouline, Colangelo, Lupkowski-Shoplik, Forstadt & Lipscomb, 2009) is argued to be a helpful tool to guide school administrators, teachers and parents. The teacher who will then receive these students in class will be sensitive to young students who are ready to advance academic material and yet who may need extra time and help in other areas, such as motor or social skills.

Most research on acceleration is carried in the form of case studies, longitudinal studies and meta-analysis (Kulik & Kulik, 1992; Rogers, 2010). It is argued that the strongest evidence for acceleration is carried by meta-analysis because it is a form of synthesis where the results of a group of studies on the same topic allow clearer conclusions to be made. Rogers (2010) carried out a synthesis of 234 studies investigating acceleration on primary and secondary schooling. One of the main outcomes gathered from the synthesis is that students who were accelerated, compared to their peers, were likely to advance academically around 5 months whilst having small social and psychological benefits. The latter consideration is crucial in that it challenges the biased view that acceleration may be a threat to students' social-emotional well-being. Moreover, in the synthesis update Rogers (2015) confirms that there is evidence that supports the idea that acceleration can impact on students' social-emotional development in a small but positive manner. However, Cross, Andersen and Mammadov (2015) argue that the latter findings need more investigation because of the methods used for data collection within the analyzed studies. For instance, the researchers report that most of the studies examining acceleration and social-emotional development include self-reported data, retrospective studies and data gathered over a short period of time that lacked evidence over a longer period of time. Therefore, the researchers concluded that there is a need for further research in this field in order to avoid drawing conclusions that could have a negative impact on students' development.

By reviewing the academic literature on acceleration, there is evidence to confirm that this strategy can be considered an empirically effective intervention for gifted and talented students that helps them achieve positive academic and social outcomes. The most important questions are, however, how and what kind of acceleration services will benefit an individual student. The following steps will serve as a pragmatic guideline for school administrators, teachers and parents to encourage the implementation of acceleration practices at their schools:

- Providing teachers with professional development opportunities to make them familiar with the practices of acceleration
- Implementing the use of assessments to identify students who may benefit from subject-based acceleration
- Developing a system of collaboration with school staff and curriculum specialists to support students at every stage of their acceleration path
- Removing barriers to implementation in avoiding biased recall of negative individual cases on acceleration by starting the conversation from data and literature on social and emotional adjustment

Cluster grouping

Cluster grouping is a widely recommended strategy in which a group of students, sharing similar achievement performance levels or interests, is provided with learning opportunities that are differentiated from a regular classroom. This strategy is often used for meeting the needs of gifted, high-achieving students who are in primary schools. Although many definitions and applications of cluster grouping have been identified in the academic literature, three components prove to be constantly present. Firstly, groups of gifted and talented students are placed in classrooms with students of other achievement levels. Secondly, teachers are required to differentiate curriculum for the gifted, high-achieving students within the clustered classroom. Thirdly, teachers who are to teach in the clustered classroom will have an interest and experience in working with gifted students.

Although cluster grouping is often associated with gifted education practice, it is important to underline that specific applications of cluster grouping consider how its use can benefit all students in the classroom. Total School Cluster Grouping (TSCG, Gentry, 2014) considers the achievement performance levels of all students in a school and, based on a reduced range of these levels, helps school administrators and teachers to create classes. One of the features of TSCG is that the model suggests a specific number of high-ability students – six to eight – to form the cluster and that the rest of the class should be heterogeneous. This means that this cluster grouping model should be viewed not only as an opportunity for the highest-achieving students but for all students in a classroom. By addressing the needs of all students and teachers, TSCG includes strategies to deal with challenging gifted students by allowing them to become academic leaders by expressing their talents among students in other classrooms. Moreover, by reducing the range of students' achievement levels, it develops the abilities of teachers to meet the individual needs of students. Finally, the fact that a cluster of gifted students is placed in a heterogeneous group allows the improvement of student achievement from all levels.

Another form of cluster grouping is what Renzulli and Reis (2014) defined as enrichment clusters within their Schoolwide Enrichment Model. Within this model, cluster grouping is viewed as a non-graded group of students who share similar interests and who gather during specific time blocks found within a school timetable to pursue their common interests. Renzulli and Reis (2014) present their Total Talent (TT) portfolio as a data collection tool that informs schools and teachers on how to plan enriched activities according to students' interests and talents or to prepare an individual education program. Facilitators, such as teachers, staff members or community members, are key in enabling the clusters to run and their involvement should be based on the same type of interest assessment. However, as the researchers have identified, one of the major issues in relation to the development of enrichment clusters is the tendency of schools to structure them as mini-courses. Whilst mini-courses are intended to teach to an audience a prescribed set of content, enrichment clusters are a learning situation that is designed to produce a product or service that will have an impact on students' lives.

To assess students' interests for cluster grouping, Renzulli's first TT portfolio can now be used within the Renzulli Learning System (RLS), which consists of an online enrichment platform in which students and teachers can access information related to a specific student. After completing a questionnaire that investigates interests, learning styles, expression styles and abilities of students, the platform takes each student to an exploration of activities based on the data gathered from the questionnaire. RLS's differentiation search engine matches the students' information to an enrichment database of 17,000 online enrichment activities and opportunities for students to develop their own personal interests. Moreover, this allows school administrators and teachers to have a bird's-eye view on the interests gathered within classrooms to plan enrichment activities both in a classroom and in non-graded classrooms.

Overall, while a limited number of studies found positive and growing effects in cluster grouping, more research is needed across different schools and with different populations. Gentry (2014) argues that comparative studies need to involve larger sample sizes so as to be able to generalize outcomes. However, the experiences found in students using Renzulli's (2014) RLS reveal positive feedback of both students and teachers when differentiating in everyday school practice.

Conclusions

This chapter is intended to help school administrators, teachers and parents to start an exploration of pragmatic strategies to

Educating gifted and talented students 85

support gifted and talented students in the classroom. Empirical evidence on enrichment programs supports the view that their design and implementation is a first practical step in reviewing school differentiation strategies. However, Subotnik, Olszewski-Kubilius and Worrell (2011) argue that, although enrichment is considered to be a frequent programming option for gifted students, there is still a lack of formal evaluation of these programs. In particular, there seems to be a gap in the literature in relation to what arises from interviews or observations of the daily implementation of these models or even what might be revealed by an investigation that looks at the transferability of these models in other school contexts. Moreover, although the focus of the academic literature leads toward strategies and models as being solely for gifted and talented students, there is potential to investigate how the same strategies apply to heterogeneous classes. Lastly, researchers have also underlined the importance of the role of the school and family relationship (Jolly & Matthews, 2012). As the researchers argue, there are four main areas in which parents express their criticisms toward gifted programming. These criticisms include a lack of confidence in the school's adequacy in developing differentiation strategies, a lack of stimulus being offered within a gifted program, distress over possible teasing or bullying toward gifted students and the perception of absent or limited communication about gifted program strategies implemented by schools. Therefore, although teachers and school administrators have the responsibility to structure and plan strategies to support gifted and talented students, the relationship between schools and families remains key in meeting every student's learning needs inside and outside the school context.

Notes

1 Subotnik, Olszewski-Kubilius and Worrell, 2011.
2 Reis and Renzulli, 2009, p. 329.
3 Feldhusen and Moon, 1992, p. 63.
4 Gagné, 1999, p. 110.
5 Plucker and Callahan, 2014.
6 Moon, Callahan, Tomlinson and Miller, 2002; Westberg, Archambault, Dobyns and Salvin, 1993; Westberg and Daoust, 2004.
7 Taber and Riga, 2006.

References

Archambault, F. X., Westberg, K. L., Brown, S., Hallmark, B. W., Zhang, W., & Emmons, C. (1993). Regular classroom practices with gifted students: Findings from the classroom practices survey. *Journal for the Education of the Gifted, 16*, 103–119.

Assouline, S. G., Colangelo, N., Lupkowski-Shoplik, A., Forstadt, L., & Lipscomb, J. (2009). *Iowa Acceleration Scale Manual: A guide for whole-grade acceleration K-8 (Manual)*. Scottsdale, AZ: Great Potential Press, Inc.

Berlin, J. E. (2009). It's all a matter of perspective: Student perceptions on the impact of being labeled gifted and talented. *Roeper Review, 31*(4), 217–223.

Betts, G. (1986). *The autonomous learner model*. Greeley, CO: Autonomous Learning.

Bloom, B. (1985). *Developing talent in young people*. New York: Ballantine.

Brighton, C. M., Hertberg, H. L., Moon, T. R., Tomlinson, C. A., & Callahan, C. M. (2005). *The feasibility of high-end learning in a diverse middle school*. University of Connecticut, National Research Center on the Gifted and Talented.

Callahan, C., & Smith, R. M. (1990). Keller's personalized system of instruction in a junior high gifted program. *Roeper Review, 13*, 39–44.

Colangelo, N., & Assouline, S. G. (1995). Self-concept of gifted students: Patterns by self-concept, domain, grade level, and gender. In F. Monks (Ed.), *Proceedings from the 1994 European Council on high ability conference* (pp. 66–74). New York: John Wiley.

Coleman, L. J., Micko, K. J., & Cross, T. L. (2015). Twenty-five years of research on the lived experience of being gifted in school: Capturing the students' voices. *Journal for the Education of the Gifted, 38*(4), 358–376.

Cross, T. L., Andersen, L., & Mammadov, S. (2015). Effects of academic acceleration on the social and emotional lives of gifted students. In Susan G. Assouline, Nicholas Colangelo, Joyce VanTassel-Baska, & Ann Lupkowski-Shoplik (Eds.), *A nation empowered: Evidence trumps beliefs that hold back America's brightest students* (Vol. 2, pp. 31–42). Iowa City, IA: Belin-Blank Center, College of Education, University of Iowa.

Csikszentmihalyi, M., Rathunde, K. R., & Whalen, S. (1993). *Talented teenagers: A longitudinal study of their development*. Cambridge: Cambridge University Press.

Delcourt, M. A. B. (1993). Creative productivity among second grade students: Combining energy, interest and imagination. *Gifted Child Quarterly, 37*, 23–31.

Feldhusen, J. F., & Moon, S. M. (1992). Grouping gifted students: Issues and concerns. *Gifted Child Quarterly, 36*, 63–67.

Educating gifted and talented students   87

Feldman, M. A., Ojanen, T., Gesten, E. L., Smith-Schrandt, H., Brannick, M., Totura, C. M. W., ... Brown, K. (2014). The effects of middle school bullying and victimization on adjustment through high school: Growth modeling of achievement, school attendance, and disciplinary trajectories. *Psychology in the Schools, 51*(10), 1046–1062.

Finn, C. E., Jr., & Wright, B. L. (2015). *Failing our brightest kids: The global challenge of educating high-ability students. Educational Innovations Series.* Cambridge, MA: Harvard Education Press.

Gagné, F. (1999). My convictions about the nature of abilities, gifts and talents. *Journal for the Education of the Gifted, 22,* 109–136.

Gentry, M. (2014). *Total school cluster grouping and differentiation: A comprehensive, research-based plan for raising student achievement and improving teacher practices* (2nd Ed.). Waco, TX: Prufrock Press Inc.

Hébert, T. P. (1993). Reflections at graduation: The long term impact of elementary school experiences in creative productivity. *Roeper Review, 16,* 22–28.

Hertberg-Davis, H. (2009). Myth 7: Differentiation in the regular classroom is equivalent to gifted programs and is sufficient: Classroom teachers have the time, the skill, and the will to differentiate adequately. *Gifted Child Quarterly, 53*(4), 251–253.

Hoekman, K., McCormick, J., & Gross, M. U. M. (1999). The optional context for gifted students: A preliminary exploration of motivational and affective considerations. *Gifted Child Quarterly, 43,* 170–193.

Houghton, C. (2014). Capturing the pupil voice of secondary gifted and talented students who had attended an enrichment programme in their infant school. *Gifted Education International, 30*(1), 33–46.

Jolly, J. L., & Matthews, M. S. (2012). A critique of the literature on parenting gifted learners. *Journal for the Education of the Gifted, 35*(3), 259–290.

Kerr, B., Colangelo, N., & Gaeth, J. (1988). Gifted adolescents' attitudes toward their giftedness. *Gifted Child Quarterly, 32*(2), 245–247.

Kitsantas, A., Bland, L., & Chirinos, D. S. (2017). Gifted students' perceptions of gifted programs: An inquiry into their academic and social-emotional functioning. *Journal for the Education of the Gifted, 40*(3), 266–288.

Kulik, J. A., & Kulik, C.-L. C. (1992). Meta-analytic findings on grouping programs. *Gifted Child Quarterly, 36,* 73–77.

Marsh, H. W., Plucker, J. A., & Stocking, V. B. (2001). The self-description questionnaire II and gifted students: Another look at Plucker, Taylor, Callahan, and Tomchin's (1997) "Mirror, mirror on the wall". *Educational and Psychological Measurement, 61*(6), 976–996.

Moon, S. M., Swift, M., & Shallenberger, A. (2002). Perceptions of a self-contained class for fourth and fifth-grade students with high to

88   Michael Cascianelli

extreme levels of intellectual giftedness. *Gifted Child Quarterly, 46*(1), 64–79.

Moon, T. R., Callahan, C. M., Tomlinson, C. A., & Miller, E. M. (2002). *Middle school classrooms: Teachers' reported practices and student perceptions* (Research Monograph 02164). Storrs: The National Research Center on the Gifted and Talented, University of Connecticut.

Nasca, D., & Davis, H. B. (1981). *Verbal behaviors of teachers of the gifted.* Unpublished manuscript (ERIC Document Reproduction Service No. ED 216 478).

Pentelbury, R. (2000). The independent learner program. In Centre for Gifted Education (Ed.), *The quest for giftedness: Proceedings of the annual conference of the Society for the Advancement of Gifted Education.* Calgary, Alberta, Canada: Centre for Gifted Education. (ERIC Document Reproduction Service No. ED 466 055).

Peterson, J. S., & Ray, K. E. (2006). Bullying and the gifted: Victims, perpetrators, prevalence, and effects. *Gifted Child Quarterly, 50,* 148–168.

Plucker, J. A. (2015). *Common core and America's high-achieving students.* Washington, DC: Thomas B. Fordham Institute.

Plucker, J. A., & Callahan, C. M. (2014). Research on giftedness and gifted education status of the field and considerations for the future. *Exceptional Children, 80*(4), 390–406.

Reis, S. M., & Renzulli, J. S. (2003). Research related to the schoolwide enrichment triad model. *Gifted Education International, 18*(1), 15–40.

Reis, S. M., & Renzulli, J. S. (2009). The school wide enrichment model: A focus on student strengths and interests. In J. Renzulli, E. J. Gubbins, K. McMillen, R. Eckert, & C. Little (Eds.), *Systems and models for developing programs for the gifted and talented* (2nd Ed., pp. 323–352). Mansfield Center, CT: Creative Learning Press.

Reis, S. M., Westberg, K. L., Kulikowich, J. M., & Purcell, J. H. (1998). Curriculum compacting and achievement test scores: What does the research say? *Gifted Child Quarterly, 42,* 123–129.

Renzulli, J. S. (1977). *The enrichment triad model: A guide for developing defensible programs for the gifted and talented.* Mansfield Center, CT: Creative Learning Press.

Renzulli, J. S., & Reis, S. (1997). *The Schoolwide Enrichment Model: A how-to guide for educational excellence.* Mansfield Center, CT: Creative Learning Press.

Renzulli, J. S., & Reis, S. M. (2014). *The Schoolwide Enrichment Model: A how-to guide for talent development.* Waco, TX: Prufrock Press Inc.

Robinson, N. M. (2004). Effects of academic acceleration on the social-emotional status of gifted students. In N. Colangelo, S. G. Assouline, & M. U. Gross (Eds.), *A nation deceived: How schools hold back America's brightest students. The Templeton*

Educating gifted and talented students 89

national report on acceleration (Vol. 2, pp. 59–67). Iowa City, IA: The Belin-Blank International Center for Gifted Education and Talent Development.

Rogers, K. B. (2002). *Re-forming gifted education: Matching the program to the child.* Scottsdale, AZ: Great Potential Press, Inc.

Rogers, K. B. (2007). Lessons learned about educating the gifted and talented: A synthesis of the research on educational practice. *Gifted Child Quarterly, 51*(4), 382–396.

Rogers, K. B. (2010). Academic acceleration and giftedness: The research from 1990 to 2008. A best-evidence synthesis. In *Proceedings of the 2008 Wallace Symposium poster session on academic acceleration* (pp. 1–6). Iowa City, IA: The University of Iowa.

Rogers, K. B. (2015). The academic, socialization, and psychological effects of acceleration: Research synthesis. In Susan G. Assouline, Nicholas Colangelo, Joyce VanTassel-Baska, & Ann Lupkowski-Shoplik (Eds.), *A nation empowered: Evidence trumps beliefs that hold back America's brightest students* (Vol. 2, pp. 19–29). Iowa City, IA: Belin-Blank Center, College of Education, University of Iowa.

Stepanek, J. (1999). *The inclusive classroom: Meeting the needs of gifted students – Differentiating mathematics and science instruction.* It's Just Good Teaching Series. Available at https://eric.ed.gov/?id=ED444306.

Subotnik, R. F., Olszewski-Kubilius, P., & Worrell, F. C. (2011). Rethinking giftedness and gifted education: A proposed direction forward based on psychological science. *Psychological Science in the Public Interest, 12*(1), 3–54.

Taber, K. S., & Riga, F. (2006). Lessons from the ASCEND project: Able pupils' responses to an enrichment programme exploring the nature of science. *School Science Review, 87*(321), 97–106.

Tomlinson, C. A., Kaplan, S. N., Renzulli, J. S., Purcell, J., Leppien, J., & Burns, D. (2002). *The parallel curriculum: A design to develop high potential and challenge high-ability learners.* Thousand Oaks, CA: Corwin Press.

Treffinger, D. (1986). Fostering effective, independent learning through individualized programming. In J. S. Renzulli (Ed.), *Systems and models for developing programs for the gifted and talented* (pp. 429–468). Mansfield Center, CT: Creative Learning.

Tyler-Wood, T., Mortenson, M., Putney, D., & Cass, M. (2000). An effective mathematics and sciences curriculum option for secondary gifted education. *Roeper Review, 22*, 266–269.

Vaughn, V. L., Feldhusen, J. F., & Asher, J. W. (1991). Meta-analyses and review of research on pull-out programs in gifted education. *Gifted Child Quarterly, 35*, 92–98.

Westberg, K. L., & Daoust, M. E. (2004). *The results of the replication of the classroom practices survey replication in two states.*

Storrs: National Research Center on the Gifted and Talented, University of Connecticut.

Westberg, K. L., Archambault, F. X., Jr., Dobyns, S. M., & Salvin, T. J. (1993). *An observational study of instructional and curricular practices used with gifted and talented students in regular classrooms* (Research Monograph 93104). Storrs: The National Research Center on the Gifted and Talented, University of Connecticut.

Chapter 5

Being a parent of gifted children and adolescents

Personal strategies to support growth

Gianluca Gualdi

The role of parents

There are no defined rules for being a good parent of a high-potential child or teenager. In fact, the profiles are so heterogeneous that only a good knowledge of the individual allows you to provide precise, timely and effective advice. Each parent must therefore identify creative and personal strategies in order to better support their child's growth.

When we talk about the parent–child relationship, we need to think of a multiple relationship, in which different aspects come into play (Figure 5.1).

In a couple we have two parents, each with their own story and parenting style. Mediation between different positions in terms of education is a crucial element for the development of the child. Couples often go into crisis when they have a child because of the difficulty of mediating their parenting position with the other figure. In many cases we also observe how a parent tends to have a secondary role (in the countries of southern Europe often at the expense of the father), which does not make co-parenting balanced.

Each parent is in a one-to-one relationship with the child. Parents of the same child can describe the child in a very different way, depending on how they live them (e.g., a parent says "when I am there he is quiet, because I let him watch the television", or "with me he discusses his emotions because I listen to him").

Generally, being a parent of high-potential children is a complex and challenging educational task (May, 2000) because of their social and emotional needs, combined with the often difficult temperament, leading parents to experience stress and

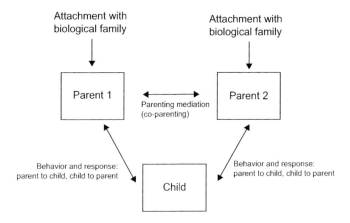

Figure 5.1 The parent has his or her own history, attachment relationships with their parent, family expectations and how they behave in the context of life.

a sense of impotence (Silverman, 1997). The sensitivity and intensity of children lead them to have deep emotional needs for which parents are often unprepared (Moon & Hall, 1998; May, 2000; Pfeiffer & Stocking, 2000; Fornia & Wiggins Frame, 2001; Morawska & Sanders, 2008, 2009a) and that are frequently confused and misinterpreted even by specialists in the field (Fornia & Wiggins Frame, 2001; Hartnett, Nelson & Rinn, 2004; Rinn & Reynolds, 2012). This aspect is related to the concern that often leads parents to turn to specialists for a psychodiagnostic assessment of the child, in order to have a picture and a greater understanding of some "out-of-sync" behavior.

Different studies (May, 2000; Fornia & Wiggins Frame, 2001) show that children can come across two types of difficulties: The first type refers to difficulties deriving from interaction with the external environment, such as the difficulty of conforming to the norms or scholastic culture; the second type mainly depends on the peculiar characteristics of the student, such as excessive self-criticism and the fear of taking risks (May, 2000; Fornia & Wiggins Frame, 2001). In these cases, valid family support can reduce the risk of "scholastic

Being a parent of gifted children   93

disaffection", the development of dysfunctional behavior and maladaptive development trajectories (Jolly & Matthews, 2012). At the same time, the parent could experience situations of embarrassment or difficulty in managing these situations, which often cause excessive anxiety or worrying, resulting in the isolation of the parent from social relationships connected to the scholastic world. Some types of high-potential children's behavior cause a sense of impotence and inability to act in parents, with the consequence of undermining the perception of their own value and role as a parent, as a supporting and caring person.

It has been found that families with a gifted child frequently provide an optimal living environment to nurture the child's "cognitive thirst"; it is important to observe how the structured environment must also take into account the affective dimension and promote interpersonal growth, an aspect that seems more complex to implement. To be optimal, the parental couple and the family environment should therefore present a high level of cohesion and mutual support, and at the same time encourage the independence of the "gifted child" to a greater extent compared to parents of "non-gifted" children (Karnes & Shwedel, 1987). This last aspect becomes particularly fundamental with adolescent children, who are often given cognitive and studious but not affective and social autonomy, creating in the child a sense of imbalance and misunderstanding of some rules. In support of this, several studies (Reis, Hebert, Diaz, Maxfield & Ratley, 1995; Rimm, 1995) indicate that families of underdeveloped underachievers are frequently characterized by conflicts and family instability.

Psychological support paths for parenting aim to support parents in their role, to promote awareness of the importance of this task, and to increase and strengthen the educational skills of the parents themselves. All this goes through a greater understanding of the child (their needs, their fears, their way of communicating, etc.), of themselves, of the relationship with them and a reflection on the educational and communicative attitudes brought into play in the relationship. With these premises it will therefore be possible to rethink new ways of behavior, expression and comparison with one's own children.

These paths are not only intended for families in particularly traumatic situations, but can be a useful path for any parent to improve their relationship with their children, family dynamics and the growth of each family member.

It is possible to identify some general indications within these support paths which can be used by parents as food for thought for the management of children with high potential.

Parents can go through stressful moments in the management of their child; however, these should not be experienced as embarrassing or repressing, but as reflections on the reasons that lead to unsuitable or dissatisfied feelings with their role.

The family also includes other figures besides the triad (mother, father and child) such as grandparents, brothers, sisters, close friends, uncles and aunts. In particular, it is important not to forget the siblings, who sometimes may not be high-potential, because they need the same attention as the other children. It is important that all the figures in the family are involved in daily emotional and affective activities, routines and exchanges.

The environment influences the personality and development of the child and therefore must be structured in such a way as to stimulate them; it must therefore be interesting, suited to the skills and abilities of the child, rich in materials and suitable for exploration. If a child is interested in geography, why not buy them a globe? In this perspective we talk about virtual knowledge and concrete knowledge. The first can be represented by a child who is interested in trains, but who has never physically ridden on one of these; the second can instead be represented by a child who is keen on trains and who rides them, travels, goes to the station with their parents, reads books on the subject and has one or more models with which they play at home. Already from this example, it is easy to understand how concrete knowledge is to be promoted more, compared to the virtual one, also in relation to the tendency toward a more kinesthetic cognitive style of the high-potential student. The child in this direction learns more, learns better and learns with more interest, and some situations (such as going to the station with the parents) can turn into pleasant moments for the whole family and are opportunities for emotional, intellectual and relational exchange.

Finally, it is important to underline how the certification of high cognitive potential highlights a series of characteristics (of strength and/or difficulty) of the individual that must be considered overall. A child with high potential can have emotional, relational or cognitive difficulties that must be considered and managed; negative situations can come into play even at a behavioral level, which are not justified by the situation. Being gifted is not a justification, but a different point of view on how to manage maladaptive or non-child behavior.

It is often useful for families to interact with others who have a high-potential child. This aspect is fundamental for the child because it allows them to interact with their cognitive peers, with whom they can share interests, passions, reasonings, moods and difficulties. Moreover, it is also possible for parents to find comfort and comparison in talking with other parents, who may experience the same difficulties or the same sense of impotence, but at the same time the same joys or strategies for action and management of such children.

Family and school

Family and school are not to be considered as two totally separate systems, as they both hold the child's cognitive, emotional and relational development. Communication between school and family is therefore essential to promote a positive growth of the student.

This aspect is central when we talk about high cognitive potential because the child often has different behaviors in the two environments. Teachers are often heard to report that the student's attention span is not very long but parents, on the contrary, watch the child read for two hours in a row. This is often linked to the fact that behavior varies depending on the environment you are in, the stimuli you receive, the rules to be respected and the attention of the adult toward the child.

What actions can then be implemented by parents and teachers to promote a school–family alliance that supports the growth of the child?

It is important to underline that clear, careful and continuous communication between family and teachers is the key for an alliance, as it consents to a shared vision of the strengths and difficulties of the child and this allows sharing of objectives, rules and management methods. Educators in the field generally agree that positive family relationships play a large part in shaping the development of the gifted child, and that the support of parents is crucial to the realization of their full potential. However, parenting a gifted or talented child may be stressful, and can strain both the parent–child relationship and sibling bonds. While it is not universally true that problems will arise, raising a gifted/talented child may present parents with unique challenges or unfamiliar situations that they did not have to tackle when raising other children in the family.

Relationships with siblings

A diagnosis of giftedness or talent may disrupt sibling relationships. There is some evidence that the siblings of gifted individuals feel greater jealousy and competition and may be less well adjusted than the siblings of non-gifted children. Gifted children may receive more attention from their parents than their siblings do, most likely because they are more demanding and require more stimulation, and this too is likely to cause competition and envy. However, it appears that difficulties among siblings are most intense soon after the label "gifted/talented" has been applied; within five years the negative effects are negligible.

It is important to remember that giftedness/talent does not cease outside of the classroom – a child will continue to be creative, interested and demanding of stimulation at home. As the child's home life plays such a large role in molding their cognitions and behavior, it is necessary to bear in mind the impact of a diagnosis of giftedness on the dynamics of the family as a whole.

Managing stress in gifted and talented children

Stress can be defined as a biological reaction to circumstances where an individual perceives a discrepancy between a situation or event and their ability to cope with that event. Everyone experiences stress, and the extent to which we suffer is related to factors such as personality and temperament. Stress in gifted children can arise from a desire for perfectionism, feelings of being "different" from their peers or concern that they cannot maintain the standard of work that is expected of them. Younger gifted children may find the classroom stressful if classmates constantly rely on them for help and support rather than asking the teacher.

Often, young children would rather ask a classmate who they perceive to be "clever" instead of admitting to a teacher that they don't know an answer. While in small measures this may benefit the self-esteem of the gifted/talented child, if it happens regularly it can cause stress because of their concern about falling behind with their own work, being caught talking when they shouldn't be or being constantly distracted by others. Busy teachers may be happy to let gifted pupils help their classmates, but often forget to convey the fact that they *know* they are helping and that the gifted child is not misbehaving or neglecting their own work.

While challenge is necessary to extend and enrich the school curriculum for gifted and talented children, it is important to ensure that the challenge is not too difficult, or too far out of the reach of the child. Anyone, if set near-impossible targets, will find the situation stressful, and it is wrong to assume that a child will relish tough challenges simply because they are gifted/talented. Extended activities should be level appropriate in order that the child does not move from the classwork they can complete with ease to a task that they struggle with, as this can be frightening and damaging to self-esteem.

Older gifted children may experience stress as they come to the senior years of the school cycle and the standard of work becomes more difficult. Suddenly the student who has always achieved straight As with no problems at all may no longer be receiving such high grades, and they need reassurance that they are not "losing their giftedness". If this problem does not arise during the final years of school, it often occurs in the early years of university, where it is no longer possible to maintain a 100% record on assignments and examinations. Such a revelation can be quite damaging to the gifted students' self-esteem and again they need reassurance and preparation for this situation before they leave school. Also, students need to be reinforced with the idea that *failure provides feedback* and is an important part of the learning process. Gifted students may be particularly reluctant to adopt this view, especially if they have an unblemished academic record, so it is necessary to highlight the *process* of learning, rather than allowing them to continually focus on the outcome.

As end-of-year and school-leaving exams loom, gifted students may experience intense stress as they struggle to live up to the high goals that they have set, to maintain their standard of work and to "prove their worth". This problem can be exacerbated by teachers and classmates who dismiss them as "having nothing to worry about". Being gifted/talented does not alleviate exam pressures and may in fact intensify them, and these students need a trusted adult to whom they can express their fears and not have these fears dismissed as groundless. Further, hard-earned results deserve due praise and should not be dismissed with comments such as "we wouldn't have expected anything less from a gifted pupil like you". It is easy to forget the amount of care and attention that a student might have put into their work, if they frequently turn in work of a high standard that appears effortless. Such comments are not only unfair to the student, but also explicitly state the weight of expectations that the student may already feel to perform well at all times and in all subjects.

Practical suggestions

- Be realistic in expectations

Gifted children can show high performance in a specific area and not in others. The parent must be aware that giftedness can be related to specific areas of learning and therefore be aware that the child may need help in other areas. A gifted child is not necessarily synonymous with success and the parent must therefore support the child in difficulty.

- Allow opportunities for creative expression

Very often, gifted students are incredibly creative. Your child may have a vivid imagination and appreciate visual and performing arts. Find an outlet for your child's creativity. The parent can identify hobbies, interests, materials and activities that promote the creative thinking of the child. In addition, courses in theater, photography or other forms of art can be strategies to promote creativity and sociability at the same time.

- Promote social skills

Gifted children can often have difficulties on the emotional and social side. In these cases the parent can propose shared readings and comments, propose reflections, use role-playing games, etc. in order to help the child put themselves in the other person's shoes. In particular, these strategies are useful with children who often fight with peers, impose their ideas, have a strong sense of justice and who appreciate debates (even if they often want "the last word" ...).

- **Learn to fail and struggle**

High-potential children often have excellent results without much effort or very quickly. This aspect influences, on the one hand, their confidence in their abilities, but on the other hand the idea of resurfacing without difficulty. If this situation continues over time, children learn to always succeed in situations and when faced with complex or more difficult tasks, they tend not to have management strategies, abandoning the task or refusing to do so. Moreover, if the tasks are simple and the self-confidence is high, errors due to distraction increase. It is therefore essential that parents support their children when they are faced with particularly complex challenges. It can also be useful to get them used to mistakes, teaching them to accept their limits.

- **Accept boredom**

How many times a day do you get bored? Like adults, children get bored too. Boredom when it's too much becomes harmful, but the right level of boredom helps to activate creative strategies. Gifted children "hate" boredom, but they must learn to live with it. It may be useful at school, "the time of boredom", or at home to help them fill in the gaps, but without providing too many activities.

- **Encourage children to explore their interests**

Each child has strengths in certain areas (e.g., math; language arts; physical, natural and social sciences; music; visual and performing arts; leadership; athletics; philanthropy). Parents and teachers can help children explore their interests. At home parents can be attentive to their child's comments and observations; they can create an environment that promotes self-expression; they can help children develop skills and interests; for example, in plant science, animal care, electronics, carpentry, mechanics, law, design and crafts; and encourage them to explore the beauty of diverse cultures – through language, poetry, stories, songs, dance, puppetry, cooking and crafts; and promote exploration and discovery.

Strategies

The right time

Gifted children can be very quiet when they are absorbed in some activities (e.g., a computer, a book, an art project or an activity that seems to have their complete attention). In these cases it may be useful to leave them their own personal space, without interrupting them while they are concentrating. It may be useful to remind them that time is running out 15 minutes before its expiration and then offer them side-by-side assistance in changing the activity.

Active listening

Gifted children often describe events with many details. In particular, they often ask for their parents' attention when telling them a story, an idea or an event. When the parent is occupied with something else, then listening is not very engaging and can be confusing. Therefore, it may be useful to identify a moment during the day when the parent actively listens (makes eye contact, makes comments and asks questions) to the child's stories, in order to stimulate the relationship and promote communication. It can also be useful to explain how not everyone has the time or desire to listen to every detail, so it can be useful for the child to summarize. Initially, it can be the parent who summarizes something first (teaching the child to do so) and then the child could be asked to summarize the story themself and could be advised to use this version with peers.

Organized disorder

High-potential children are often disorganized and leave great confusion around them. It can be helpful to help them organize the room, the games and the activities they perform, proposing examples for rearranging (e.g., using colored boxes, practical examples, labels), then letting the child identify the most effective strategy.

Bibliotherapy

Have your child read books with main characters who also have unique abilities and uneven development.

References

Fornia, G. L., & Wiggins Frame, M. (2001). The social and emotional needs of gifted children: Implications for family counseling. *The Family Journal*, 9(4), 384–390.

Hartnett, D. N., Nelson, J. M., & Rinn, A. N. (2004). Gifted or ADHD? The possibilities of misdiagnosis. *Roeper Review*, 26, 73–76.

Jolly, J. L., & Matthews, M. S. (2012). A critique of the literature on parenting gifted learners. *Journal for the Education of the Gifted*, 35(3), 259–290.

Karnes, M. B., & Shwedel, A. (1987). Differences in attitudes and practices between fathers of young gifted and fathers of young non-gifted children: A pilot study. *Gifted Child Quarterly*, 31, 79-82.

May, K. M. (2000). Gifted children and their families. *The Family Journal, Counseling and Therapy for Couples and Families*, 8(1), 58–60.

Moon, S. M., & Hall, A. S. (1998). Family therapy with intellectually and creatively gifted children. *Journal of Marital and Family Therapy*, 24(1), 59–80.

Morawska, A., & Sanders, M. R. (2008). Parenting gifted and talented children: What are the key child behaviour and parenting issues? *Australian and New Zealand Journal of Psychiatry*, 42(9), 819–827.

Morawska, A., & Sanders, M. R. (2009a). An evaluation of a behavioural parenting intervention for parents of gifted children. *Behaviour Research and Therapy*, 47, 463–470.

Morawska, A., & Sanders, M. R. (2009b). Parenting gifted and talented children: Conceptual and empirical foundations. *Gifted Child Quarterly*, 53, 163–173.

Pfeiffer, S. I., & Stocking, B. V. (2000). Vulnerabilities of academically gifted students. *Special Services in the Schools*, 16(1–2), 83–93.

Reis, S. M., Hebert, T. P., Diaz, E. P., Maxfield, L. R., & Ratley, M. E. (1995). Case studies of talented students who achieve and underachieve in an urban high school (Research Monograph 95120). Storrs, CT:

University of Connecticut, National Research Center for the Gifted and Talented.

Rimm, S. (1995). *Why Bright Kids Get Poor Grades and What You Can Do about It*. New York: Crown Trade Paperbacks.

Rinn, A. N., & Reynolds, M. J. (2012). Overexcitabilities and ADHD in the gifted: An examination. *Roeper Review*, 34(1), 38–45.

Silverman, L. K. (1997). Family counseling with the gifted. In N. Colangelo & G. A. Davis (Eds.), *Handbook of gifted education* (2nd ed., pp. 382–397). Needham Heights, MA: Allyn & Bacon.

Part II

Supporting gifted students in school

Chapter 6

Watching the plants grow
Understanding giftedness in science

Keith S. Taber

Introduction

This chapter considers what might be meant by suggesting that someone, and, in particular, a school-age learner, is gifted in science, and offers some suggestions for how such a student can best be supported by teachers and parents. The term 'gifted' can have some unfortunate associations (for example, that some people have been blessed in some particular way, and so, by implication, others have not), but as it is widely used it will, with qualification, be adopted here. The qualification is that the term gifted will be understood and used in a particular way.

Giftedness and high ability in science

The notion of giftedness informing this chapter might be described as 'contextual' and, when used in relation to educational provision, 'pragmatic'. It is *contextual* in the sense that it is not considered that there are some people who simply 'are' *gifted*, or indeed 'are' (absolutely and for all time) *gifted in science*, but rather that a judgement of giftedness relates to a person relative to a particular learning context (or a particular area of practice, such as working in a particular scientific field at some particular stage of its development). If Isaac Newton or Marie Curie could somehow be transferred into a contemporary university science department today, then they would be unlikely to be able to perform as productive scientists, let alone be perceived as scientific geniuses. Perhaps such a time-travel scenario is unfair to them, as they would likely still have the *potential* to be great scientists, but unable to show this potential as they would not have been inducted into the current ideas and practices of science. Yet, as Thomas Gray (1751) long ago recognised, history has ignored countless people with the *potential* for greatness but born into circumstances where their potential was never nurtured and fulfilled to enable notable achievement.

So judgements of giftedness are made within particular contexts, and this links to the *pragmatic* notion of a learner being seen as gifted within a specific educational context. In some teaching contexts there are students that have existing levels of knowledge, understanding, and skills, such that curriculum and teaching suitable for their classmates would not be appropriate for them (Taber, 2007b). Suitable and appropriate are here related to the idea of educative provision capable of supporting a learner's substantive development. There are times in an educational programme where it may be useful to have students practise existing skills and apply previously mastered knowledge in order to reinforce learning, and perhaps increase accuracy and speed of recall. We might associate terms such as 'exercises' and 'drill' with such activities. However, an educational programme that only (or mainly) provided these types of experiences would offer little basis for learning new skills, developing new insights, and opening up new areas of knowledge. Educative experiences are those that support these types of qualitatively novel – for that learner – developments.

A well-designed curriculum or programme of study should be educative in this sense. However, it is possible for a student to be placed in a programme which is a poor fit, such that it is experienced mainly as review and drill, rather than offering anything substantially new. (It is also possible for some students to be in inappropriate programmes because they have insufficient skills and background knowledge to effectively engage with teaching and access learning. That is an equally serious concern, but not the focus here.)

School classes are by their nature made up a range of students with different current levels of attainment, and of readiness and potential for making further progress, and therefore teachers are faced with planning teaching that can concurrently be educative for students with quite different characteristics. In practice, it may often be the case that classes, and indeed prescribed curriculum, may be designed with a notional 'typical' learner in a particular grade level in mind, in which case it is quite possible that there may be some students in the class not readily challenged. Whilst these learners can certainly complete work effectively and successfully (at least if they can be motivated to engage with it), they benefit very little from activities that are genuinely educative for many of their classmates.

It is these students that are considered here to be usefully identified as gifted: those that will not be challenged and developed by curriculum, teaching, and learning activities, considered suitable for their peers. Such a judgement is contextual in a number of ways. For example, development of intellectual skills is not uniform, and a seven-year-old who would be considered gifted in their year group might later (through no blame on the child) have ceased to count as gifted by 14 years of age. Equally, the opposite might be true. People have different strengths. Learners who are bored and find no stimulation or challenge in mathematics classes that stretch most of their classmates might attend literature classes, with the same group of peers, and be fully engaged in work that is pitched at a level that is educative for them (again, or vice versa).

Perhaps there are some children who we should just consider 'gifted' as they are exceptional all-rounders – but we also find children and young adults who are clearly gifted in some curriculum contexts but not others. It has also been widely reported that some learners are twice (or more) exceptional in the sense of having some particular learning difficulties that slow their progress in some aspects of school, whilst showing exceptional abilities in particular areas (Sumida, 2010; Winstanley, 2007). An example might be a student who, because of specific learning difficulties, struggles to produce high-quality written work, but when engaged in oral discussion is able to demonstrate highly complex and sophisticated thinking and argumentation skills not reflected in their writing. Clearly, it would also be possible for the true potential of gifted learners with, say, short-sightedness or hearing impairment not to be apparent unless those conditions were diagnosed and addressed to allow the learners to properly access teaching.

It should also be pointed out that, as with most human characteristics, giftedness is not binary (gifted/not gifted) but can be seen to lie on a continuum – or more correctly, given that it is multifaceted, to occupy a point in an imaginary multidimensional space. Given this contextual and pragmatic perspective, references to learners who are 'gifted in science' have to be understood here to mean those judged to need particular provision in the sciences, or some aspects of science, at this particular time, given the curricular programme they would normally be expected to follow.

The reference to some aspects of science is important as it is possible to be considered gifted in physics but not biology, or even to show exceptional insight in, say, understanding chemical reaction mechanisms and suggesting synthetic routes, whilst not standing out from the class when carrying out calculations in physical chemistry. Ideally we would want *all students* in *all classes* to at *all times* be tasked with work that is sufficiently challenging to potentially catalyse their development, whilst simultaneously being sufficiently supported to engage productively and so to make clear progress in their learning (Taber & Riga, 2016). Such an ideal may not be feasible when teachers are working with large classes and have limited time for preparing or sourcing classroom resources, or if they are expected to teach through an impoverished pedagogy (if teacher-led exposition to the whole class is not complemented and co-ordinated with dialogic class discussion, enquiry activities, group-work, etc.), but it is a worthy aspiration, even when an unrealistic expectation.

Giftedness is clearly associated with high intelligence, which is often measured by IQ tests. However, there have been various attempts to offer broader and more inclusive understandings of intelligence (Gardner, 1993; Sternberg, 2009), and, given the range of characteristics useful to achievement in science, the gifted scientist is not simply someone with a very high IQ (Gilbert & Newberry, 2007).

What makes for a gifted scientist?

Given a contextual notion of giftedness, what makes for giftedness in science needs to be understood in the context of the nature of science. Clearly, being a successful student in science will involve developing a good deal of scientific knowledge, being able to understand and apply abstract ideas (such as laws, principles, models, and theories), and effective deductive thinking to draw logical conclusions. The latter is itself a contextual matter as although deductive logical has an algorithmic nature – in principle it could be programmed into a machine – the appropriate conclusions that can be drawn from a particular data set always depend upon the theoretical framework being employed. That is, data only become evidence within a particular theoretical perspective.

So, students that are successful in science and can proceed to scientific careers will tend to have at least these qualities in common. However, scientists who become recognised as leaders among their peers (in their professional context) tend to notice things that others do not consider as significant, and imagine possibilities that their peers have not considered (Kuhn, 1970). They tend to be especially inquisitive, and to not be satisfied with standard and accepted answers.

Examples might include the likes of Darwin who built a new central perspective for the science of biology based on his own extensive field observations, and reports he collected of observations from anatomists, farmers, pigeon fanciers, and others; and Einstein who based some of his most influential work on the outcomes of imagining what it would be like to travel on a beam of light. Nobel laureate physicist Richard Feynman highlighted the inquisitive nature of successful scientists as people who are not satisfied with surface explanations and who engage with problems as puzzles to be solved – such as his role in identifying the cause of the NASA Challenger Space Shuttle failure. When working as a young scientist on the Manhattan Project (that developed the first US atomic weapons), Feynman treated the locks on the cabinets where secret documents were stored as puzzles to be solved. In 1959 Feynman gave a talk that in retrospect can be seen as a manifesto for a new area of science developing machines on a scale comparable to molecules. He imagined the possibility of what we now call nanoscience or nanotechnology.

Those who make the greatest breakthroughs are often those who are prepared to entertain alternatives to what might be considered as accepted truths: what if the universe is not centred on the Earth; what if the continents are not fixed features of the Earth's surface; what if all life on Earth is related by descent from one common ancestor? For example, Einstein disregarded the common-sense notion that the measured speed of light would depend on one's own speed (as in everyday experience: when a car travelling at 55 km/h overtakes a lorry travelling at 50 km/h it is moving at a speed of 5 km/h relative to the lorry), and explored the consequences of assuming the seemingly illogical

110 Keith S. Taber

premise that the speed of light is the same for all observers, regardless of how fast they are moving. This led to the general theory of relativity, which has since been extensively tested and found to fit observations.

Spotting gifted science students

These considerations suggest two complementary ways to identify those we might consider gifted in science among children and young adults – in terms of the ease of meeting curriculum goals, or in terms of potentially indicative characteristics. A teacher should be concerned about any student who seems to succeed in class activities without needing to stretch themselves intellectually. School is not meant to be like adult work in one important sense. In an employed position we generally (if not always) want workers to be working within their comfort level where they can succeed in assigned tasks. We do not want to be operated upon by the surgeon who has never undertaken this new procedure before – even if the experience will be educative for the doctor. We are unlikely to want to buy a recording of the concerto being played by an artist who is currently struggling to add it to her repertoire, even if it reflects an important phase in her artistic development.

Most parents would be concerned to be told that because of unexpected staffing changes in the school, their child will now be taught history by a mathematics teacher who has not taught history before but who has some capacity in her timetable to take on an additional class, even if they knew she was a good maths teacher, had always liked history, and was really committed to doing a good job. Yet a learner's job in school is just like this: to work at something they are not currently competent in, and develop new skills or areas of expertise. We want the teacher to have expertise in the curriculum being taught, but if a student already has that expertise, then the demands need to be raised. So, teachers should always be seeking to ensure all students are being suitably challenged to move beyond their current levels.

It may not always be easy for parents to apply the same criteria. A child who is consistently achieving very high grades in school, and does not seem to need to make a great effort to do so, may be insufficiently challenged: but the parents will not have a full picture of the context of performance and the level at which assessment is being pitched. Moreover, in many education systems, study in the lower grades is less clearly discriminated across subject boundaries, and there may be few obvious indicators to parents of how challenging different curriculum areas are found to be. Some gifted children, if by no means all, may be perfectionists, and so may report subjective evaluations of needing to work harder in a subject (or even of 'failing'), despite objectively performing at exceptional levels. The most able often have greater metacognitive awareness and can be better at recognising their limitations than many of their peers. There are, however, some other potential indicators that may prove useful to parents, as well as teachers, looking to identify those potentially gifted in science.

Scientific interests

Whilst interest does not necessarily indicate ability – it is quite possible for someone to be fascinated with an academic area without becoming accomplished in it – some gifted learners may demonstrate intense, perhaps almost obsessive, interests in specific areas of science. Science is not an activity which at its heart is about compiling facts (even if the layperson may sometimes think otherwise), but it does depend on data as the basis for building scientific knowledge.

So, it is not unusual for young people to take an interest in, say, dinosaurs, but a gifted youngster may start to develop an encyclopaedic knowledge of where fossils of particular species have been found, what those species ate, when they are believed to have lived, and so forth. This is just one example, and the focus could be volcanoes, or galaxies, or trees, or spiders, or minerals, or computer chips, etcetera. The point of relevance is that the knowledge built up is extensive, and systematic, and not just a scattering of isolated facts. Systematic here means relating specific examples to formal typologies and schemes of classification, which involves abstraction and often links to theoretical considerations.

The particular interest may be quite specialised but may be strong enough to encourage consideration of a career in the relevant science, and to motivate wider studies that will facilitate this. Systematicity is a characteristic of scientific activity, and might be seen as one quality needed for a 'scientific mind': so

112 Keith S. Taber

a precocious tendency to organise and categorise and systematise (whether in a traditional hobby such as stamp or coin collecting, or by sorting the loose buttons in a sewing box) at an early age may indicate an aptitude for science.

Observational skills

Classifying requires observation skills, and these also link to habits of mind. Children generally have similar perceptual abilities, but they do not all notice the same things. To, with William Blake (1863), 'see a world in a grain of sand', one has to first notice the grain and imagine that it is worth close inspection. A typical garden may be visited by a range of bee species of quite different size and appearance, but this needs to be noticed (unless it has been pointed out), which only happens if attention is paid. When the bath is emptied, the water flows down the plug hole – but how does this happen? Someone who had never paid attention might suspect a continuous body of water in the bath and pipe that slowly drops in level. Does a child like to wait and watch as the water exits the bath and see how (usually!) a vortex forms and changes shape and apparent speed as the system evolves?

What if a child is asked to describe moss? Do they offer more than 'it is a green material sometimes found on rocks and wood'? Do they describe the texture, and comment on variations? Have they used a magnifying glass, or even a microscope, to resolve the single mass into discrete plants? Do they see 'moss' as a unitary notion, or have they (as with bees) recognised this as a category that encompasses subdivisions? Have they noticed that sometimes, but not always, the mosses have stalks rising above the main body of the plants?

Such observations can certainly be considered protoscientific. In some areas of science, expertise allows the scientist to make observations that the layperson is not equipped to make. For example, although some fossils may be obvious in their natural context (albeit our observations are flavoured by the theoretical perspective we adopt – at one time many people dismissed fossils as simply decorative patterns found in rocks), the professional palaeontologist or anthropologist may be able to identify small fossil fragments, on a beach for example, which are not readily discriminated from the background material by the untrained observer.

Awe and wonder

The reader may suspect that the previous sentence betrays a fallacy in the suggestion that gifted young scientists can sometimes be identified by the habits of observation: after all, observation can be trained. Learning to see cell organelles down a microscope, for example, is not simply a matter of being observant: it is a process of coming to interpret observations in relation to canonical scientific knowledge. The student learns to see the nucleus, the chloroplast, the mitochondria, and so forth.

This is true – we can learn to make observations if we are prepared to put in the time and attention required. The sports fan who regularly watches televised football matches learns to see patterns in play, and to spot rule infringements, and tactical shifts. Likely, some people have greater propensity than others to learn to observe these things, but what is required is the motivation to engage in close observation, regular feedback (from expert commentary, and the decisions made by match officials), and the commitment of a good many hours of engagement in the activity!

Motivation to engage in close and extended observations is therefore an issue here. Some children take time to look closely at the moss, or to wait watching till the bath empties, and many do not. Scientists often have a sense of awe and wonder about the natural world when many (if certainly not all) other adults may take natural phenomena for granted. Young children tend to have this sense of awe and wonder, but (for whatever reason) differ in the extent to which they retain this as they grow. The five-year-old that spends an hour staring at how the cloud formations slowly shift in the sky may be considered quaint, but if a 15-year-old does the same, they risk being judged as retarded or lazy: after all, once you've seen a few clouds and learnt that they move across the sky and change shape over time, what else is there to see?

Yet the scientist often retains that childlike sense of wonder in nature, and does not take natural phenomena for granted but retains a strong aesthetic pleasure in the night sky, or the reflections on a lake, or the apparently metallic lustre of a beetle's cuticle. The child examining yet another acorn or yet another oak leaf may be genuinely enjoying the beauty of these apparently simple, but actually highly complex, structures, with their commonality of form (every oak leaf is the same ...) but unique individualities (... whilst every oak leaf is different). One characteristic that marks effective scientists is the tenacity to commit to and stick with a project and see it through: single-mindedness and patience, and confidence that perseverance can be rewarded, can be useful habits of mind for the future scientist.

Inquiring minds

Observing, and noticing, are therefore important, although not enough by themselves to make a future scientist. The scientific mind does not just make and classify observations, but seeks to explain them. Why does the moss tend to grow here, and not there? Why does its extent change over the year? Why does it only sometimes produce those stalks with their capsules at the top – and is there a pattern to when this happens (when it gets warmer; or after heavy rain)?

Again, children often ask many questions when young – perhaps to the point where parents get frustrated, and may often not know the answers. Most parents would struggle to offer valid answers to the multitude of potential questions curious children can ask: Why is the sky blue? Why does water make you wet? Why do we have to eat? Why can't you see the stars in the daytime if the sun only blocks a tiny part of the sky? Why do onions smell?

Perhaps especially relevant are those questions that are based on some form of comparison between parallel observations: Why do dogs bark, but cats do not? Why do some trees grow taller than others? Why can't we breathe underwater, if fish can? Why does the grass grow back after it has dried out, but many other plants die off? If babies can live healthily on milk, why do I need a varied diet? ... These questions may indicate the development of the basis for that most important scientific technique: control of variables.

Scientists not only ask questions; they also the critique answers received and then seek deeper levels of understanding. Some children may be happy enough to be told that cats do not bark because they meow instead, but others may see that response as little more than deflecting the question. Explanations that are little more than tautology (gem stones have regular shapes because they are crystals) or based on classification (a kangaroo has a pouch because it is a marsupial) may offer only momentary satisfaction. In science the most satisfactory answers are those that fit within an existing conceptual framework, and ideally can be subsumed under widely applicable principles and theories (such as conservation of energy and momentum, natural selection, and the molecular theory of matter). This may be reflected in the gifted young scientist with their tendency to systematise.

As has been clear since at least the time of Aristotle, there can be different kinds of explanations, and for the inquisitive mind a satisfactory explanation may be multi-levelled. That some trees shed their leaves, and others do not, could be explained by suggesting there are two classes of tree: deciduous and evergreen – but that will not satisfy the inquisitive mind that wants to follow-up the original question with a 'but why?' Older people often need to wear glasses because people tend to get more long-sighted as they age: 'but why?' (And, indeed, 'how?') Toilet cleaner is often blue because it contains copper salts which are often blue: 'but why' are copper salts often blue? Just as parents may be tempted to respond to the question of why it is time for bed with a 'because I say so', they may sometimes have little to offer the inquisitive child's questions ('why does Mars have two moons and Earth only one?') beyond 'that's just the way it is'.

Science itself seeks to ultimately understand just the way things are, and often proceeds, like the inquisitive child, in steps such that each explanation can in turn be seen as an explicandum to be explained by a more nuanced or subtle answer. When adolescent students were questioned by an interviewer taking on the role of the inquisitive child (by asking a series of questions, such that the student's explanation for a phenomenon was itself subjected to a 'but why …'-type follow-up question) it seemed that learners differ considerably in terms of how quickly they reach a 'that's just the way the world is' position (Watts & Taber, 1996). The 'natural attitude' (Schutz & Luckmann, 1973), that people come to accept many of the regularities in the world as given and not needing further explanation, is probably a necessary coping strategy – but the scientific attitude avoids too readily accepting that something is 'just natural' and the gifted young scientist is likely to always be seeking to understand (rather than just know), and is seldom satisfied for long with the first level of explanation encountered.

Testing truths

So gifted young scientists show a critical faculty not to simply accept the word of an authority, but to want to think things through and be persuaded for themselves. They are likely to try planting seeds from imported fruits that they have been told 'will not grow here' to see for themselves. They are less likely to take on board dubious common notions with currency among their peers: for example, noticing that sometimes they can see the moon in the daytime sky, so it is not only a night-time object. They may even want to test out for themselves what seem perfectly sensible notions: *we all know* that plants grow too slowly for us to directly observe the growth (thus the attraction of those films made with time-lapse techniques which accelerate such processes). If they read, or hear reported, that the direction in which the circulation occurs when the bath drains is different in the Northern and Southern hemispheres, they may question this idea by imagining adjacent baths emptying with their plugs either side of the equator, and asking themselves, 'how could such a small difference in position matter – is there a possible mechanism?' This thought experiment requires running a mental simulation, informed by their intuitions about how things work – a technique sometimes employed by professional scientists.

In general terms, 'the enquiring mind' may be understood as one that asks questions, but *in science* enquiry goes beyond asking to seeking to find out by empirical investigation – such as perhaps seeking to make a sequence of observations over successive bathing episodes to test whether what they see is consistent with the (actually false) claim that the rotation is always in the same sense North (or South) of the equator. Indeed, the precocious young scientist may well accelerate the programme of research by spending a few hours repeatedly filling and emptying the bath to collect data.

The laboratory of the imagination

Carrying out experiments to test ideas is only possible when someone can imagine possibilities to test. One would need to imagine the two baths at the equator before it would be possible to set up a real test. All scientific discoveries occur twice: first, they are discovered as a possibility in the mind of a scientist, and then in the conclusions drawn from the result of experiments set up to test that possibility (Taber, 2011). If being discovered only as a possibility seems a weak kind of 'discovery', then we might instead say that scientific discoveries are *invented* prior to discovery. Genes, germs, molecules, double bonds, neutrons, Neptune, and so forth were all first invented as ideas (discovered in the mind) before they were found in nature. Of course, science is an iterative process, so observations invite explanations ... that invite testing, and so further observations .... Once the idea of germs has been invented, and experimental work has confirmed that the germs idea seems a good explanation for some diseases, then we might consider that previously available data can now be considered evidence of germs: but that is a reconstruction.

It is now thought that Galileo Galilei observed and recorded the position of Neptune – but it was more than two centuries later that Neptune (having been imagined as an additional planet, and predicted, and looked for) was discovered. Indeed, many scientific discoveries are smeared out over time. Humphry Davy discovered potassium, but it only became potassium after he had conceptualised and tested out his initial discovery of what appeared a previously unknown metallic substance. Moreover, it only became potassium *as characterised today* after many decades of further measurements, some of which relied on ideas and instruments (e.g. X-rays, radioactive decay) that had not been 'invented' in Davy's lifetime (Taber, 2019).

Some of the great discoveries of science have arguably only completed the first stage – discoveries in imagination still being tested empirically. Evidence for the Higgs boson (sometimes called the 'God particle') has now been obtained, but it is very indirect evidence of data from one set of instruments (albeit at CERN, the extensive European centre for nuclear research) interpreted in term of complex models and assumptions. Gravitational waves seem to have now been detected, but about a century after Einstein imagined the possibility. Darwin discovered (the idea) of the common ancestor of all life on Earth; but like the Big Bang, and superstrings (and the extra dimensions of reality assumed to be associated with them), and the dark energy and WIMPS (weakly interacting massive particles) said to make up much of the mass of the universe, and many other conjectured scientific objects and events, the accretion of convincing evidence for the referent is an ongoing process.

118 Keith S. Taber

The history of science is indeed littered with imagined discoveries of conjectured entities that are now no longer widely considered to really exist: phlogiston, N-rays, caloric, polywater, cold fusion. In many spheres of human activity such episodes might be considered errors and failures, but in science the testing of such ideas, and finding them an inadequate match to our observations of the world, is considered an essential component in making progress (Popper, 1989). Even if it seems idealistic to expect scientists to always be pleased when their pet ideas seem to have been discredited, the scientific attitude is to value the resulting advance in knowledge above any personal disappointment.

It is well recognised that science relies upon deductive logical, and scientists must be rational thinkers: but it is just as true that science relies on imagination, and productive scientists must be creative thinkers. The gifted young scientist needs to adopt high levels of abstraction and systems-thinking. Imagination is one of the most important faculties for the young scientist, and the child gifted in science is likely to have a very active imagination. We should encourage gifted young scientists to generate alternative conceptualisations for testing, rather than prematurely closing down judgement and committing to an enticing idea that may later have to be modified or discarded.

Watching paint dry – or plants grow

There is an idiom that 'it was like watching paint dry'. The implication intended is that some activities are as boring as watching paint dry: something that is a slow process with nothing to see. The gifted young scientist might well take that as a challenge. Paint drying involves a transition between two very different states, but a gradual transition – and presents a challenge for understanding, and indeed setting up conditions for productive observation. This is certainly a suitable focus for scientific enquiry.

Everyone knows that plants grow, but, as suggested above, also that this is a slow process that cannot be directly observed. Everyone knows this – apart, that is, from a gifted youngster who has invested substantial periods of time observing how the tendrils of a climbing plant, such as a passionfruit vine, behave when the breeze brings them into contact with something offering potential support. Observation is said to be theory-laden (Basu, 2003), which does not necessarily mean that we only ever see what we expect to see, but certainly does mean we often miss what we cannot imagine to be the case. The careful observer will report having directly observed the tendrils both visibly lengthen and coil during one episode of direct observation: something that is invisible to the casual observer without the curiosity to wonder how the plant manages to climb, the imagination to consider possibilities, and the patience to seek out the conditions expected to be productive for observation (where a tendril is periodically making contact with or rubbing against a suitable supporting structure) and spend time waiting to see what will happen. This is patience that is supported not only by the epistemic hunger to acquire an understanding, but also the desire to see for oneself.

Implications for teachers

Teachers are professionals who should be entrusted to make decisions about the education of young minds in their care. Yet, the scope teachers actually have to design and implement curriculum varies considerably, and with an increasing 'accountability' culture in many educational contexts, and the importance placed on formal 'high-stakes' tests that often have highly specified learning objectives, many teachers may be offered limited scope to shift from prescribed schemes of work.

One approach to working with gifted learners is to advance them by moving them ahead of their age group. This is sometimes successful, but is not always appropriate. For one thing, this requires a consistent approach – there is little point accelerating gifted students in this way only for them to later reach a point where acceleration to the next stage is not possible and they need to repeat a year. This is also a solution that assumes giftedness is a global evaluation: timetables seldom allow easy acceleration in some but not other subjects, and progress in intellectual development may not be matched by emotional maturity or physical development. Such approaches may be questioned on social grounds as developing peer relationships (which may be disrupted by advancement, and may be harder to initiate with older peers) are as important to personal growth as classroom learning.

An alternative approach to meeting the needs of gifted students not challenged by the curriculum is to offer suitable extra-curricular activities. These can include 'Olympiad'-type competitions (Oliver, 2017; Petersen, Blankenburg, & Höffler, 2018) or special programmes put on by university outreach initiatives (Horner et al., 2018) or enrichment programmes especially designed for gifted science learners (Taber, 2007a). These types of provisions can be very valuable, as gifted learners often find them enjoyable, and appreciate they are doing something special – and indeed they may report that they appreciate being challenged to think at a deeper level (Taber & Riga, 2006). However, unless care is taken (Kulbago, Mulvey, & Alamri, 2016), Olympiad-type events, based on *competition* between teams or individuals, could give a particular impression of science that may be considered unbalanced – for example, from feminist critiques (Bentley & Watts, 1987). Activities that require students to visit universities or special study centres may have particular impact, but may raise questions about access unless efforts are made to encourage gifted learners from all backgrounds, and provide funding (for travel and so forth) for those who do not come from families readily able to make such investments in extra-curricular activities. Indeed, gifted learners in some groups, such as indigenous learners in some national contexts, may need particular targeting or support to allow them to access gifted programmes (Franco, Verjovsky, Cisneros, & Torre, 2017; Rosin, Cutler, & Carson, 2017).

The terms 'extra-curricular' and 'enrichment' reflect the main reason why this approach to meeting the needs of gifted learners should not be a primary strategy. If gifted learners are only challenged in science by attending extra activities, then this equates to spending their time in science lessons as 'treading water', constantly waiting for the rest of the class to catch up. It is clearly not right that we make students attend standard classes which are not matched to their needs, and then suggest that if they actually want educative experiences, they need to *also* commit additional time to something extra. *Extra*-curricular provision should offer enrichment beyond, and in addition to, a suitably challenging core curriculum, and suitable opportunities should be available to all those keen on science, not just the gifted.

The teacher with some gifted young scientists among a more diverse class therefore needs to consider other options, and this will mean some level of individualisation in learning. One approach might be a form of compacting (Renzulli, Smith, & Reis, 1982), where in each topic those considered gifted in that context (perhaps identified by topic-specific pre-tests) spend part of their time working with the rest of the class, but some time on different work. Perhaps the teacher provides expositions of new ideas and content for all, and whilst most of the class undertake learning activities to review and reinforce what has been presented, the more gifted learners are set more challenging activities such as exploring nuances of theory and more complex applications.

The principle here, as outlined earlier, is that all students should be sufficiently challenged and suitably supported. Many students find new abstract ideas met in science as alien and counter-intuitive, and need to be given opportunities to work with those ideas in relatively straightforward ways as they become familiar and slowly mastered. Gifted learners tend to make the abstractions more easily, and sometimes actually find they match their own intuitive notions or possibilities they have already imagined, so they do not need as much time in the familiarisation stage, and they are ready to test, develop, and apply the ideas in contexts not suitable for most of their peers.

It seems that perhaps whilst most of the class are working on basic activities to consolidate teaching, gifted learners could be undertaking project work, enquiry activities, problem-solving, discussion work, developing an artefact (such as a model), and so forth. Yet, there is a danger here. Educational research shows the value of dialogue, argument, enquiry, etc. in learning, and such activities can be very engaging. It would clearly not be appropriate if a group of gifted learners were undertaking such activities whilst most of the class were doing book-based exercises that might appear inherently (and, to students, obviously) less exciting. Providing educative provision for gifted learners should not appear to be rewarding the clever children with more interesting work. So similar pedagogy should be used for all the students, but honed to meet the needs of different groups. One principle that has been suggested, based on the educational ideas of Vygotsky (1978), is that teachers might plan learning activities with the most gifted learners in mind initially, and then consider the types of supports and additional resources and bridging activities that would make the work accessible and manageable for other learners in the class (Taber & Riga, 2016).

Another potentially valuable strategy is to enrol gifted learners in supporting the learning of others in the class, by giving them roles in micro-teaching episodes, peer tuition, and the development of new learning resources. This must not be (or be seen to be) on the basis of 'you have finished the work, so you can help someone else'. Rather, whilst supporting other learners is a valuable side-effect, the logic here is to provide gifted learners with a meaningful activity that has a clearly useful purpose, but which enables them to explore and apply their new learning in more challenging ways (Taber, 2015). It is widely recognised that using knowledge to teach others requires in-depth examination of that knowledge, and how it is connected, and how it might be understood: and so is potentially educative for the teacher. Gifted students must appreciate they are undertaking work that is valuable for them as well as others, and the teacher needs to be sensitive to learners' preferences – some gifted children will revel in explaining things to others; some may not be comfortable in face-to-face teaching roles, but may be happy building a teaching model or designing a poster. An alternative, more subtle, approach that can sometimes be employed is to design group-work (e.g. different groups in the class design posters summarising different themes in a topic) where the gifted learners can provide intellectual leadership without being highlighted as having a particular role in the activity.

Implications for parents

Parents may have limited input into the formal teaching their child experiences, but are much less constrained than teachers in developing the 'curriculum' of out-of-school activities. In some national contexts it is usual for concerned parents (or at least those with the resources) to seek to supplement formal schooling with evening or Saturday schools and private tutors to reinforce and drill school learning. This is probably not healthy for children in general, and certainly is likely to be resented by gifted students who may already find school lessons too pedestrian. In some other cultures there is (again, usually in those groups with the resources to afford to do so) a very well-meaning attempt to provide a rich learning environment for children by signing them up for a wide range of intellectual, artistic, and sporting activities to fill up their free time. This may not be an ideal approach to helping children develop either.

Watching the plants grow   123

That is certainly not to criticise parents who wish to offer their children the opportunity to try out kayaking, pony riding, judo, dance, additional languages, piano, and the rest. The gifted young scientist may well benefit greatly from visiting museums, science centres, zoos, botanic gardens, and observatories, and attending science and technology clubs, and so forth. However, there are two important provisos. Gifted learners often tend to develop particular interests, and may focus on them in depth (where many of their peers may soon become bored, and flit from one activity or hobby to another). It is useful if parents can *introduce* young children to a wide range of clubs and activities and give them a taste of what is on offer. However, children will only benefit from activities they are motivated to commit to, and it is counter-productive to push them to continue with activities they are not enjoying. Gifted students may be better supported by enabling them to spend extensive time in a small number of activities where they genuinely become immersed than pushing them to spend time in activities where they are not keen to engage. Boredom is perhaps a particular turn-off for gifted people, and – especially as children approach adolescence – nothing is as boring as being somewhere you would rather not be, doing something that does not interest you, because someone else thinks it is good for you.

The second point is also related to the disdain for being bored, in that gifted learners are unlikely to be bored when left to their own devices. Imagination is core to scientific work, and the gifted child is usually very good at developing imaginative play. Scientific successes often depend on periods of intense practical activity, interleaved with periods of mulling things over – whilst walking, or swimming, or taking a bath – and distraction and focus elsewhere. It is important that children, and arguably especially gifted children, have some regular free time that is not organised for them by adults or older siblings. This allows them to identify and develop interests, and to follow them up in depth. It gives time for wondering (and wandering) – and so for the kinds of aesthetic experiences described above: really spending time looking at the shape and structure of a tree, watching how the cloud formations slowly shift, staring at the evening sky to see how more and more stars slowly become visible as it gets darker. The noticing can lead to simple enquiry activities such as following the ants back to find the nest, tracing the course of a stream ....

Parents can support their gifted child by being tolerant and supportive of their interests. Sometimes this may mean encouraging a child to develop alternative activities which use resources more carefully – it is not environmentally friendly to keep filling a bath with clean water, just to empty it again – so how can we model this system less wastefully? Ideally, a parent may not want hundreds of decaying leaves brought into the house or a telescope left set up by the lounge window, but it may be possible to negotiate compromises between the child's tendency to see the home environmental as part of the 'laboratory of the world' and a desire for more domestic normality. Perhaps a box room or shed can be used for ongoing investigations that would be compromised by tidying away. Perhaps there is a small area of the garden that can be given over to activities that may be more productive in germinating ideas than edible or pretty plants. Perhaps the most important thing a parent can do is maintain the balance of showing a genuine interest in the gifted child's activities and ideas, without seeking to take over leadership of them. The parent may sometimes have a better idea of what is likely to produce results than the child, and should certainly offer guidance if consulted, but the gifted youngster will likely both appreciate, and benefit more from, being left to dwell on challenges, and recognise and appreciate their own failures (which often motivate thinking again, and trying something else), than being offered the shortcuts of received wisdom.

In conclusion

In science itself, eventual success derives from habits of being amazed; wondering; questioning; periods of deep reflection; imagining and even day-dreaming; repeated testing; close and prolonged observation; coming, sometimes slowly, to recognise that an idea is wrong; accepting the implications of empirical evidence over pet hunches and assumptions; and seeing failure as the successful elimination of one alternative, and so as an impetus for going again. The gifted young scientist will benefit from educative activities, whether at school or at home, that encourage the development of such habits.

References

Basu, P. K. (2003). Theory-ladenness of evidence: A case study from history of chemistry. *Studies in History and Philosophy of Science Part A, 34*(2), 351–368. doi:10.1016/S0039-3681(03)00022-0.

Bentley, D., & Watts, D. M. (1987). Courting the positive virtues: A case for feminist science. In A. Kelly (Ed.), *Science for girls?* (pp. 89–98). Milton Keynes: Open University Press.

Blake, W. (1863). Auguries of innocence. Available at: www.poetryfoundation.org/poems/43650/auguries-of-innocence.

Franco, A. G., Verjovsky, J., Cisneros, R. A., & Torre, G. D. L. (2017). Science education for female indigenous gifted students in the Mexican context. In M. Sumida & K. S. Taber (Eds.), *Policy and practice in science education for the gifted: Approaches from diverse national contexts* (pp. 158–169). Abingdon, Oxon: Routledge.

Gardner, H. (1993). *Frames of mind: The theory of multiple intelligences* (2nd ed.). London: Fontana.

Gilbert, J. K., & Newberry, M. (2007). The characteristics of the gifted and exceptionally able in science. In K. S. Taber (Ed.), *Science education for gifted learners* (pp. 15–31). London: Routledge.

Gray, T. (1751). Elegy written in a country churchyard. Available at: www.poetryfoundation.org/poems/44299/elegy-written-in-a-country-churchyard.

Horner, D. S., Viale, G., Grazioli, C., Pirovano, L., Micklos, D., & Plevani, P. (2018). Talented students and motivated teachers: An interactive and synergistic tandem to design innovative hands-on learning practices in biosciences. In K. S. Taber, M. Sumida, & L. McClure (Eds.), *Teaching gifted learners in STEM subjects: Developing talent in science, technology, engineering and mathematics* (pp. 145–156). Abingdon, Oxon: Routledge.

Kuhn, T. S. (1970). *The structure of scientific revolutions* (2nd ed.). Chicago, IL: University of Chicago Press.

Kulbago, L., Mulvey, B. K., & Alamri, A. (2016). The US Science Olympiad experience interplay between competition and cooperation. In K. S. Taber, & M. Sumida (Eds.), *International perspectives on science education for the gifted: Key issues and challenges* (pp. 166–178). Abingdon, Oxon: Routledge.

Oliver, M. C. (2017). Science Olympiad students: A case study of aspiration, attitude and achievement. In M. Sumida & K. S. Taber (Eds.), *Policy and practice in science education for the gifted: Approaches from diverse national contexts* (pp. 147–157). Abingdon, Oxon: Routledge.

Petersen, S., Blankenburg, J., & Höffler, T. (2018). Challenging gifted students in science: The German Science Olympiads. In K. S. Taber, M. Sumida, & L. McClure (Eds.), *Teaching gifted learners in STEM*

126   Keith S. Taber

subjects: Developing talent in science, technology, engineering and mathematics (pp. 157–170). Abingdon, Oxon: Routledge.

Popper, K. R. (1989). *Conjectures and refutations: The growth of scientific knowledge* (5th ed.). London: Routledge.

Renzulli, J. S., Smith, L. H., & Reis, S. M. (1982). Curriculum compacting: An essential strategy for working with gifted students. *The Elementary School Journal, 82*(3), 185–194. doi:10.2307/1001569.

Rosin, V., Cutler, S., & Carson, S. (2017). 'Seaing' the difference: Turning policy into practice in a secondary science gifted programme in marine science. In M. Sumida & K. S. Taber (Eds.), *Policy and practice in science education for the gifted: Approaches from diverse national contexts* (pp. 34–47). Abingdon, Oxon: Routledge.

Schutz, A., & Luckmann, T. (1973). *The structures of the life-world* (R. M. Zaner & H. T. Engelhardt, Trans.). Evanston, IL: Northwest University Press.

Sternberg, R. J. (2009). Toward a triarchic theory of human intelligence. In J. C. Kaufman & E. L. Grigorenko (Eds.), *The essential Sternberg: Essays on intelligence, psychology and education* (pp. 33–70). New York: Springer.

Sumida, M. (2010). Identifying twice-exceptional children and three gifted styles in the Japanese primary science classroom. *International Journal of Science Education, 15*(1), 2097–2111.

Taber, K. S. (2007a). *Enriching school science for the gifted learner.* London: Gatsby Science Enhancement Programme.

Taber, K. S. (2007b). Science education for gifted learners? In K. S. Taber (Ed.), *Science education for gifted learners* (pp. 1–14). London: Routledge.

Taber, K. S. (2011). The natures of scientific thinking: Creativity as the handmaiden to logic in the development of public and personal knowledge. In M. S. Khine (Ed.), *Advances in the nature of science research: Concepts and methodologies* (pp. 51–74). Dordrecht: Springer.

Taber, K. S. (2015). Affect and meeting the needs of the gifted chemistry learner: Providing intellectual challenge to engage students in enjoyable learning. In M. Kahveci & M. Orgill (Eds.), *Affective dimensions in chemistry education* (pp. 133–158). Berlin; Heidelberg: Springer.

Taber, K. S. (2019). *The nature of the chemical concept: Constructing chemical knowledge in teaching and learning.* Cambridge: Royal Society of Chemistry.

Taber, K. S., & Riga, F. (2006). Lessons from the ASCEND project: Able pupils' responses to an enrichment programme exploring the nature of science. *School Science Review, 87*(321), 97–106.

Taber, K. S., & Riga, F. (2016). From each according to her capabilities; to each according to her needs: Fully including the gifted in school science education. In S. Markic & S. Abels (Eds.), *Science education towards inclusion* (pp. 195–219). New York: Nova Publishers.

Vygotsky, L. S. (1978). *Mind in society: The development of higher psychological processes.* Cambridge, MA: Harvard University Press.

Watts, M., & Taber, K. S. (1996). An explanatory gestalt of essence: Students' conceptions of the 'natural' in physical phenomena. *International Journal of Science Education, 18*(8), 939–954.

Winstanley, C. (2007). Gifted science learners with special educational needs. In K. S. Taber (Ed.), *Science education for gifted learners* (pp. 32–44). London: Routledge.

Chapter 7

Teachers' conceptions of giftedness and gifted education

An international perspective

Daniel Hernández-Torrano

Introduction

There is widespread agreement that giftedness is a socially constructed concept and that conceptions of giftedness vary across contexts, cultures, and countries. In this regard, and despite the relatively large body of research on Western conceptions of giftedness, little is known about this topic in other parts of the world. A growing number of studies in the last decades have examined the conceptions that Asian people hold about giftedness in East Asian, Southern Asian, and Southeastern Asian regions. However, no studies on the conceptions of giftedness in Central Asia have been conducted to date. The purpose of this cross-sectional study was to examine secondary teachers' conceptions of giftedness and gifted education in Kazakhstan, the largest economy of the region, and currently involved in a modernization process of its education system placing gifted education as a vehicle for improving the competitiveness of education, developing national human capital, and reforming society. Two-hundred and twenty-nine Kazakhstani secondary school teachers in North Kazakhstan and Akmola regions completed a 24-item questionnaire designed by the authors to measure their conceptions about the nature of giftedness, the identification of gifted students, the purpose of gifted education, and the provisions for gifted students. Descriptive and inferential analyses were conducted to study overall teachers' conceptions and the effect of teachers' years of teaching experience and type of school (mainstream vs. gifted) on their conceptions. Discussion of the limitations of the study, directions for future research, and educational implications of the study for Kazakhstan, Central Asia, and elsewhere are provided.

Teachers' conceptions

The study of teachers' conceptions about giftedness is a critical issue in the field of gifted education. This idea is based on the assumption that teachers play a fundamental role in the identification of students for gifted services, as they are in a unique position to recognize students' competence and potential in the classroom beyond the information provided by achievement and performance tests (Chan, 2000; Gagné, 1994; Hunsaker, 1994; McBee, 2006; Pierce et al., 2007). Also, there is empirical evidence that teachers' conceptions of giftedness and gifted education influence classroom practices and therefore the opportunities to facilitate students' talent development and academic excellence (Berman, Schultz, & Weber, 2012; Missett, Brunner, Callahan, Moon, & Price Azano, 2014).

Although the conceptions of teachers may vary according to multiple personal and contextual factors, a review of the literature on this topic allows us to draw some general trends. First, there is widespread agreement that teachers tend to hold traditional conceptions about the nature and manifestation of giftedness (i.e., scores in standardized tests above a certain cut-off score) and typically define giftedness in terms of high IQ, strong reasoning skills, good memory, and a general storehouse of knowledge (e.g., Moon & Brighton, 2008). Moreover, other studies have evidenced that teachers also support broader conceptions of giftedness beyond mental abilities, including facets such as being original, imaginative, curious, and goal oriented, and having high expectations (e.g., Kim, Shim, & Hull, 2009; Schroth & Helfer, 2009).

Second, the literature collectively suggests that educators support the use of multiple criteria to identify gifted students (Brown et al., 2005; García-Cepero & McCoach, 2009; Schroth & Helfer, 2008). Nevertheless, educators seem to be more favorable toward certain methods of identification, such as standardized tests, teacher nominations, portfolios, performance assessments, and observations, in detriment to others (e.g., parent nominations and student nominations) (Schroth & Helfer, 2008). In addition to that, discrepancies in the identification procedures preferences between different teachers' profiles have been reported in the literature. For example, Schroth and Helfer (2008) found teacher nominations to be the most effective identification method for regular teachers, while standardized tests are viewed as the most valid tool for gifted specialists. Controversially, Brown et al. (2005) evidenced that gifted teachers are more favorable to the expanded identification procedures that go beyond standardized testing than regular teachers.

Third, teachers are generally supportive of different approaches to gifted education. Specifically, teachers tend to believe that acceleration is a particularly appropriate strategy to address the academic needs of gifted students (e.g., Gallagher, Smith, & Merrotsy, 2011; Hoogeveen, Van Hell, & Verhoeven, 2005; Siegle, Wilson, & Little, 2013). However, teachers seem to have neutral to slightly negative views about the effects of acceleration on the emotional and social dimensions of students and are concerned about the pressure exerted by teachers and parents on the accelerated students (Gallagher et al., 2011; McCoach & Siegle, 2007; Siegle et al., 2013). In this context, Siegle et al. (2013) found that teachers were more favorable toward certain forms of acceleration, such as advanced programs and curriculum compacting, and less supportive of other acceleration strategies, such as early admission to kindergarten and whole-grade skipping. In addition, teachers can be slightly concerned with the elitist connotations of other gifted education approaches, such as ability grouping (Gallagher et al., 2011; McCoach & Siegle, 2007).

Fourth, some characteristics of students are believed to influence teachers' conceptions of giftedness. For example, teachers are more likely to nominate for gifted services students who are male (Bianco, Harris, Garrison-Wade, & Leech, 2011; Endepohls-Ulpe & Ruf, 2005; Lee, 2002), belong to the dominant cultural, linguistic, or ethnic group (Elhoweris, Mutua, Alsheikh, & Holloway, 2005; McBee, 2006; Tenenbaum & Ruck, 2007), have average to high socioeconomic status (Elhoweris, 2008; McBee, 2006; Moon & Brighton, 2008), and do not have any associated learning disabilities (Bianco, 2005; Bianco & Leech, 2010). In addition, some characteristics of teachers have also shown an effect on their perceptions of giftedness and gifted education. Thus, teachers' conceptions vary depending on teacher credentials (i.e., general, special, gifted education), preparation (i.e., preservice, in-service), and years of experience (e.g., Bianco & Leech, 2010; Carman, 2011; Speirs Neumeister, Adams, Pierce, Cassady, & Dixon, 2007).

Fifth, there is widespread agreement that giftedness is a socially constructed concept and that conceptions of giftedness vary across contexts, cultures, and countries (Pfeiffer, 2012; Phillipson & McCann, 2007; Sternberg, 2007). Generally speaking, the conceptions of giftedness in Western cultures are based on the idea that people are born with different levels of intelligence and ability, while Eastern cultures assume that these differences are due to the way people acquire and use their intelligence (Niu & Brass, 2011). In this regard, and despite the relatively large body of research in Western countries on conceptions of giftedness and the characteristics that people think "make a child gifted", little is known about this topic in other parts of the world. A growing number of studies have examined the conceptions that Asian people hold about giftedness during the last decade. Most of these have focused on people from East Asian countries such as China (e.g., Chan, 2008), Japan (Matsumura, 2007; Shibata & Forbes, 2009), and Korea (Kim et al., 2009; Lee, Cramond, & Lee, 2004). Also, some researchers have explored this issue in Southern Asia (e.g., Sharma, 2012) and Southeastern Asia (see Phillipson, 2007). However, no studies on the conceptions of giftedness in Central Asia have been conducted to date.

Conceptions of giftedness in Central Asian countries (i.e., Kazakhstan, Kyrgyzstan, Tajikistan, Turkmenistan, and Uzbekistan) are relevant worldwide because of their geostrategic location and the political and social changes that have occurred since their independence from the Soviet Union. Kazakhstan is a particularly interesting case for several reasons. First, Kazakhstan is the largest economy in the region. Second, the country is currently involved in a deep process of modernization of its education system to meet the demands of a knowledge-based economy combining the advantages of the national education system and the best of international research and education practices. And third, Kazakhstan has recently placed gifted education as a vehicle for improving the competitiveness of education, developing national human capital, and reforming society (see Yakavets, 2014). Successful implementation of gifted education policies will largely depend on teachers' knowledge, practices, and attitudes toward gifted education. Therefore, a greater understanding of current Kazakhstani school teachers' conceptions and practices related to gifted education could provide valuable information to design educational opportunities for talent development and overall school improvement in Kazakhstan and elsewhere.

The purpose of this research was to examine secondary teachers' current conceptions of giftedness and gifted education in Kazakhstan. More specifically, the study aimed to answer the following research questions:

- What beliefs do teachers hold about the manifestation and nature of giftedness?
- What is the rationale and purpose for providing gifted education services according to teachers?
- How do teachers think gifted students' characteristics and needs can be identified?
- How should we provide education services for gifted students according to teachers?
- How do teachers' conceptions of giftedness differ across years of teaching experience and type of school (mainstream vs. gifted)?

Methodology

Methods

A survey questionnaire was developed by the researchers to examine teachers' conceptions of giftedness in Kazakhstan in a five-stage process. First, researchers reviewed the general body of research on teachers' conceptions of giftedness and initially generated 60 items. Second, 10 researchers working in the field of gifted education (professors and doctoral students) were invited to participate in a content validation process of the questionnaire assessing the quality of each item in terms of adequateness, relevance, certainty, and favorability to measure the construct it was intended to measure (e.g., conceptions about the nature and manifestation of giftedness). Based on the feedback provided by the content validators, 36 items were selected, revised, and included in a pilot version of the questionnaire. Third, a sample of 100 teachers were asked to complete the 36-item pilot version of the questionnaire indicating the degree to which they disagreed or agreed with these items on a seven-point Likert scale (1 = completely disagree, 7 = completely agree). Fourth, a series of four principal component analyses with varimax rotation were conducted (1) to reduce the data into a small set of components to facilitate the interpretation of teachers' conceptions of giftedness in terms of the nature of giftedness, the identification of gifted students, the purpose of gifted education, and the provision of education services for gifted students, and (2) to determine the set of items to be retained in the final version of the questionnaire. The Bartlett's test of sphericity and the Kaiser-Meter-Olkin (KMO) test of sampling adequacy were computed for the four principal component analyses to determine the appropriateness of the data for these analyses in the items of the questionnaire. Components were extracted and selected on the basis of eigenvalues, a careful examination of the scree plot, and substantive considerations regarding the structure and interpretability of the different solutions (Kaiser, 1974; Pallant, 2010). Fifth, based on the interpretation of the results of the principal component analyses, 24 items were ultimately retained in the final version of the questionnaire to measure teachers' conceptions of giftedness in terms of the nature of giftedness (six items), the identification of gifted students (six items), the purpose of gifted education (six items), and the provision of education services for gifted students (six items). In addition to this information, a series of items was included in the questionnaire to collect information about the socio-demographic background of the participants, including teachers' gender, years of teaching experience, type of school, and previous participation in gifted education trainings.

Participants

Eight urban schools (four in the North Kazakhstan region, four in the Akmola region) were selected using convenience sampling procedures and all teachers of these schools were invited to participate in the study based on their availability. A total of 229 Kazakhstani secondary school teachers (200 females) completed the final version of the questionnaire. The sample reported an average of 18.61 years of teaching experience (SD = 11.81). The majority of the participants taught language subjects (40.9%), while the rest taught natural sciences (24.4%), social sciences (8.4%), arts (4.4%), or other subjects (21.4%). Among them, 52.8% were teaching in mainstream schools, and 47.2% were teaching in specialized schools for gifted students. Of the 229 secondary school teachers, 60.6% reported never having participated in training activities related to gifted education, while 39.4% indicated they had participated in courses on provision for gifted students.

Procedures and data analysis

Teachers completed the questionnaire individually or in small groups. One of the authors of the paper oversaw all sessions that lasted approximately 30 minutes. Permission to conduct this study and access participants was granted by local educational authorities and by the principals of the schools. All respondents were asked to provide written consent before participating in the study. The names of the participants and the schools were not collected or associated with the research findings in any way to protect participants' identity and confidentiality of the data and to prevent socially desired responses. Descriptive analyses were conducted to examine overall teachers' conceptions of giftedness and gifted education in Kazakhstan and inferential analyses were conducted to examine statistical differences on teachers' conceptions of giftedness and gifted education by teachers' years of experience, and type of school (i.e., gifted/mainstream). The assumptions of independent observations, homogeneity of variances, and normal distributions of the dependent variable for each group were checked and met.

Results

Teachers' conceptions about the manifestation and nature of giftedness

The majority of teachers in the sample agreed that giftedness is a quality characterizing people who can learn very fast and who possess extraordinary thinking and reasoning skills (item 5; M = 5.83, SD = 1.20). In addition, along with unique cognitive features of the gifted, teachers highly supported the non-cognitive manifestations of giftedness (item 1, M = 5.80, SD = 1.29). On the contrary, less support was provided to the hypothesis that gifted students are those students who suffer from a mismatch between the school curriculum and their educational needs (item 6; M = 4.96, SD =1.77).

In terms of the debate "giftedness as a set of static traits" vs. "giftedness as a developmental state", contradictory results were evidenced. On the one hand, most teachers shared the perception that giftedness is a human quality that can manifest differently and be developed within a specific environment. More specifically, teachers generally agreed with the idea that giftedness is not a steady concept, i.e., it can be developed through curriculum modifications and content adaptation (item 2; M = 5.69, SD = 1.25). Similarly, teachers tended to agree that giftedness can be promoted if a gifted child is supplied with appropriate technical facilities and supported in the environment (item 3; M = 5.37, SD = 1.55). On the other hand, when teachers were asked if giftedness is genetically hereditary, the degree of their agreement was rather high as well (item 4; M = 5.21, SD = 1.74).

Teachers' conceptions about the identification of gifted students

In general, teachers tend to believe that multiple criteria for the identification of gifted students are needed. Thus, the respondents agreed that gifted students should be identified by relying not only on standardized tests, but also through observations in their classroom environment to capture their authentic performance (item 8; M = 5.74, SD = 1.12). Moreover, educators supported the position that teachers and parents play an important role in the identification of gifted students (item 11; M = 5.64, SD = 1.15). Being aware of the importance of gifted identification, teachers showed only slight agreement that there is no need to establish a "gifted status" for students identified as gifted in the classroom (item 9; M = 4.95, SD = 1.65) and agreed to the least extent with the idea that the procedures to identify unmet educational needs of gifted students are similar to those used to identify unmet needs of other students in the regular classroom (item 10; M = 4.35, SD = 1.39). Accordingly, teachers demonstrated moderate agreement with the statements that identification should determine if a child is gifted or not (item 12; M = 5.12, SD = 1.48) and that identification should result in nominating gifted children for enrichment opportunities and other gifted services (item 7; M = 5.37, SD = 1.15).

Teachers' conceptions about the purpose of gifted education

Teachers in the sample tended to agree that gifted education should facilitate the development of students' strengths and interests and assist students to achieve excellence in their areas of talents. This was manifested in the highest scores for the items that referred to gifted education as the provision of opportunities, resources, and encouragement to develop their talents as fully as possible (item 16; M = 6.36, SD = 0.82) and gifted education as the cultivation of a broad, diverse range of strengths and interests, which will help students achieve excellence (item 17; M = 6.26; SD = 0.92). In addition, teachers seemed to agree to a similar extent that gifted education should also serve the purpose of developing the intellectual elite of the nation and promoting the welfare and vitality of society, as evidenced by comparatively high scores in the statements that refer to gifted students as a valuable source for the country's human capital development (item 15; M = 6.09; SD = 0.02) and to the purpose of gifted education as a vehicle to develop the leaders of the future in various fields (item 18; M = 6.08; SD = 1.14). In contrast, teachers were less likely to agree with the idea that gifted education should serve to match the needs of gifted students to the characteristics of the curriculum, as represented by lower means in the item that stated the purpose of gifted education should be as an educational instrument to match students who otherwise experience a mismatch with the curriculum they receive (item 14; M = 5.14; SD = 1.38). Interestingly, teachers scored lower in the item indicating schools should avoid divisions between gifted and non-gifted students because this raises equity concerns compared to the other items in this subscale (item 13; M = 4.74; SD = 1.82), reflecting the idea that teachers have little concern about the segregation of gifted students in special classes.

Teachers' conceptions about the provision of education for gifted students

Responses evidenced that teachers generally agree that gifted education should provide a variety of opportunities for talent development which are often not included in the standard school curriculum (item 22; M = 6.10, SD = 0.99). This belief seems to be based on a shared position that gifted children need special education programs because of their unique characteristics (item 24; M = 5.94, SD = 1.17). In order to achieve that, teachers seem to agree to a similar extent with two related statements. First, teachers believe that the regular curriculum should be flexible and specifically tailored for gifted children to address their needs (item 23; M = 5.83; SD = 1.09). Second, teachers in the sample also had positive views toward the idea that curricular and instructional approaches to gifted education are determined by what gifted learners are capable of or interested in and motivated for (item 19; M = 5.74; SD = 1.06). Interestingly, teachers seemed to be slightly in favor of having special programs for gifted students and less positive about the adaptation of curriculum and instruction to the needs of gifted learners on an individual basis in the regular classroom (item 20; M = 5.59; SD = 1.31). In fact, teachers did not seem to have particular concerns with the segregation of gifted students and their placement into special programs, i.e., having them educated separately from their non-gifted peers (item 21; M = 4.28; SD = 2.02).

Effect of years of teaching experience and type of school

A series of two one-way between-groups multivariate analyses of variance (MANOVA) with Bonferroni correction were conducted to analyze the effect of respondents' years of teaching experience and type of school on their conceptions of giftedness and gifted education. The fixed factors were teachers' years of teaching experience (0–10 years, 11–20 years, 21–30 years, and 30+ years of teaching experience) and type of school (mainstream, gifted). The dependent variables were the mean scores of the 24 items of the survey questionnaire. Preliminary assumption testing was conducted to check for normality, linearity, univariate and multivariate outliers, homogeneity of variance covariance matrices, and multicollinearity, with no serious violations noted.

Years of experience

Results evidenced a significant effect of years of teaching experience on overall teachers' conceptions of giftedness and gifted education: F (24, 157) = 1.564, $p < .05$; Wilk's Λ = 0.807, partial η^2 = .19. Univariate analysis evidenced significantly different responses across groups with different years of teaching experience in item 4 ($p = .008$, $\eta^2 = .04$), item 9 ($p = .27$, $\eta^2 = .05$), item 17 ($p = .019$, $\eta^2 = .06$), and item 21 ($p > .001$, $\eta^2 = .11$). Bonferroni post-hoc tests revealed that most experienced teachers (30+ years) scored significantly higher than least experienced teachers (0–10 years) in items 4 and 17, significantly higher than relatively experienced teachers (11–20 years) in item 9, and also significantly higher than very experienced (21–30 years) in item 17. All of this suggests that, compared to teachers with less teaching experience, most experienced teachers believed to a greater extent that giftedness is genetically inherited; gifted people are a valuable source for the country's human capital development; and informal procedures such as recommendations of parents and peers should be used together with more formal procedures (i.e., testing) for the identification of gifted students. Moreover, relatively experienced teachers (10–20 years), very experienced (21–30 years), and the most experienced (30+ years) scored significantly higher than the least experienced teachers (0–10 years) in item 21, suggesting that more experienced teachers support to a significantly greater extent the segregation of gifted students compared to the least experienced teachers.

Type of school

A significant effect of type of school on overall teachers' conceptions of giftedness and gifted education was found: $F (24, 147) = 1.751$, $p < .05$; Wilk's $\Lambda = 0.778$, partial $\eta^2 = .22$. Univariate analyses evidenced that teachers working in specialized schools for gifted students rated six items of instruments significantly higher than teachers working in mainstream schools: item 4 ($p = .003$; $\eta^2 = .05$), item 13 ($p = .002$; $\eta^2 = .03$), item 18 ($p = .002$; $\eta^2 = .03$), item 19 ($p < .001$; $\eta^2 = .08$), and item 21 ($p = .002$; $\eta^2 = .05$). Overall, these results suggest that teachers working in specialized schools tend to believe to a greater extent that giftedness is genetically inherited; gifted identification should help to determine if a student is gifted or not and to make decisions about the admission and placement of students in gifted services; and gifted students should be educated separately from their non-gifted peers.

Discussion

The purpose of this study was to examine secondary teachers' conceptions of giftedness and gifted education in Kazakhstan in terms of the nature and manifestation of giftedness, the procedures to identify gifted students, the purpose of gifted education, and the provisions for education services for gifted students.

In general, the results of this study suggest that Kazakhstani teachers hold broad conceptions about the nature and manifestation of giftedness, the identification of gifted students, and the purpose of gifted education. Four findings support this assumption. First, teachers seem to hold multidimensional conceptions of the nature of giftedness that comprise, on the one hand, a set of higher mental abilities that are expressed in the ability to learn at a faster rate than their classmates, to master complex ideas, and to reason deeply, and on the other hand, a cluster of non-cognitive traits that facilitate the development of cognitive skills, as has been evidenced elsewhere (e.g., Kim et al., 2009; Schroth & Helfer, 2009). Second, teachers in Kazakhstan consider that both an innate ability and strong environmental support play an equally important role in terms of the way giftedness and its related facets are manifested and developed, in line with other research studies conducted in Western countries (e.g., García-Cepero & McCoach, 2009; Moon & Brighton, 2008). Third, teachers in our sample considered that gifted identification should serve two interrelated purposes. On the one hand, identification procedures should serve as a discrimination tool to determine which students are gifted and which ones are not (i.e., labeling). On the other hand, the identification should serve as a nomination instrument to determine which students should have access to special programs for gifted students (i.e., placement). In order to address this dual purpose, teachers in Kazakhstan believe that the identification of gifted students requires using multiple and various procedures beyond standardized intelligence and achievement tests, including performance monitoring in natural contexts (e.g., classroom), and the opinion of parents and teachers (Brown et al., 2005; García-Cepero & McCoach, 2009; Schroth & Helfer, 2008). Interestingly, teachers in this study also indicated that these instruments should be different from the procedures that are commonly used to determine the strengths of non-gifted students in the classroom. Fourth, teachers overall considered that one of the main objectives of gifted education in Kazakhstan remains the capitalization of the superior abilities of gifted students for the good of the whole society and increased progress, as it was traditionally in the Soviet education system (e.g., Grigorenko, 2000, p. 735), but results also suggest that considerably more attention is being paid to the personal development and growth of the students in the context of modern Kazakhstan.

In contrast, this study suggests that Kazakhstani teachers maintain more traditional and narrower conceptions regarding the provision of educational services for gifted students. Thus, one of the most interesting findings was the apparent tolerance of teachers in Kazakhstan about the segregation of gifted students in special classes and schools. In this sense, teachers in our sample did not consider that educating gifted and non-gifted students in separate groups and in special programs (e.g., ability grouping) raises equity concerns. This seems to contradict the results found in studies conducted in other countries, where teachers are often reluctant to separate students by ability because of the elitist connotations implied in such provisions (e.g., Gallagher et al., 2011; McCoach & Siegle, 2007). A plausible explanation for teachers' preference of providing special services for gifted students separated from non-gifted students may be that the institutional tradition of segregated special provision for exceptional children and adolescents inherited from the Soviet education system is still dominant in Kazakhstan[1] (Rouse, Yakavets, & Kulakhmetova, 2014). Thus, although inclusive education policies have been promoted in recent years to eliminate exclusionary practices that are a consequence of discriminatory policies, provisions, and attitudes to diversity in race, language, ethnicity, religion, gender, and ability (OECD, 2014), these are still in an experimental stage and, more importantly, have remained outside the range of action of the specialized schools for gifted students under the belief that education for gifted students is still useful to improve the competitiveness of the economy and the education system in Kazakhstan, as indicated above. In addition to this, teachers believed that schools should provide students with opportunities for talent development which are not typically provided in the regular classroom, such as academic Olympiads. Academic Olympiads are intellectual competitions at regional, national, and international levels in which participants are exposed to advanced tasks and problems in a specific domain (mathematics, physics, chemistry, informatics), which continue to be extremely popular among post-Soviet countries. Olympiad winners and finalists receive scholarships and access higher education without taking the national entry exam and teachers may be rewarded with bonuses and better career prospects. Success in academic Olympiads is also seen as a source of pride and satisfaction for schools and a means to further the reputation of the country (Jeltova & Grigorenko, 2005; Ushakov, 2010).

One more noteworthy outcome from this study was that more experienced teachers and teachers working in special schools for gifted students tend to hold more traditional views of giftedness and gifted education, not only related to the provision of educational services for gifted students, but also related to the nature and manifestation of giftedness and the purpose of gifted education. This conclusion stems from the greater support of more experienced and gifted school teachers for the genetic and inherited nature of giftedness, the segregated education of gifted students, and the idea that gifted students are a valuable resource for the country's development, when compared to other groups with less teaching experience and those working in mainstream schools. Two interesting inferences emerge from these results. First, Hernández-Torrano and Tursunbayeva (2016) revealed that the demographic characteristics of the students (i.e., gender, ethnicity, and socioeconomic status) did not influence teachers' conceptions of gifted students in Kazakhstan. However, this study revealed that certain characteristics of teachers, namely teaching experience and teacher credentials (i.e., working in a special school for gifted students), do have an effect on their conceptions of giftedness and gifted education. Second, traditional conceptions of more experienced teachers found in this study partially contradict previous studies, which revealed less stereotypical thoughts about the gifted in more experienced teachers (Carman, 2011; Megay-Nespoli, 2001). Similarly, the more traditional conceptions of teachers working in special schools for gifted students contrast with the literature, which suggests that teachers who have been trained to recognize advanced development have experience in teaching gifted students and sufficient time to observe children's talents, and are more sensitive and accurate in identifying talented students and responsive to their needs (Borland, 1978; Chan, 2000; Gagné, 1994; Siegle & Powell, 2004). Collectively, traditional conceptions of more experienced teachers and those from gifted schools could potentially be explained since more experienced teachers were educated at the time when beliefs about the fixed and inherited nature of skill were more widespread. In addition, because of the place of their employment, teachers from special schools are likely to be more supportive of the segregated education of these students.

Limitations and future research

The purposeful sampling procedures used in this study limit the generalization of the findings. In addition, the majority of the sample consisted of language teachers, which may have affected the results of this study. Studies in the future should analyze the effect of teaching area in teachers' conceptions of gifted and gifted education. Also, the sample consisted mainly of urban teachers. Because of the differences between rural and urban schools in Kazakhstan in relation to teacher quality, available resources, and academic achievement of students (OECD, 2014), and the dissimilarity in beliefs and gifted education practices between rural and urban teachers (e.g., Howley, Rhodes, & Beall, 2009; Lawrence, 2009), future studies should analyze differences in teachers' conceptions of gifted education and gifted education in both contexts.

Conclusion

All in all, the results of this study suggest that Kazakhstani teachers hold broad conceptions of giftedness in terms of the nature and manifestation of giftedness, the identification of gifted students, and the purpose of gifted education. This is positive insofar as it means that teachers conceptualize giftedness as a malleable set of capabilities and potentialities, both cognitive and non-cognitive, that can and should be developed for the benefit of society and the individual. However, the results of this study suggest that teachers in Kazakhstan offer only limited opportunities for gifted education and talent development in schools. In general, teachers consider that education for gifted students should be provided in specialized schools. Therefore, it is reasonable to think that gifted students who do not study in these schools have fewer opportunities to develop their talents. Besides, teachers generally support gifted education through activities outside the classroom, mostly in the form of preparation to compete in academic Olympiads, which also limits the opportunities of gifted students with average or low academic achievement and those who are less interested in this type of competition. This was particularly true with regards to more experienced teachers and those working in special schools for gifted students. In this context, preservice and in-service teacher education programs should aim to motivate teachers to provide other forms of gifted education beyond pull-out programs, such as enrichment opportunities, authentic learning, and mentorship, both inside the classroom and outside to cultivate a broader, more diverse range of strengths and interests and to help students to achieve excellence in their chosen areas.

Note

1 Students identified as gifted in Kazakhstan generally study at one of three types of special schools for highly able students. First, there are specialized schools (e.g., gymnasiums, lyceums) with more advanced curricula that provide opportunities to talented students for in-depth study of one or more areas of specialization – typically in mathematics and physics, but also in social sciences, humanities, and arts. Second, gifted students may attend one of the 34 elite schools for gifted students under the scientific and educational institution Daryn (Giftedness) Research and Practical Center, which admit students based on results from entry exams and receive considerably higher levels of funding than mainstream schools. In addition, they benefit from better buildings and facilities and greater levels of autonomy to hire teaching staff and develop their own educational programs. Third, the most prestigious schools for gifted students are Nazarbayev Intellectual Schools (NIS), which were recently created on the initiative of the President of the Republic to change the way education is delivered to gifted and talented secondary-aged children and as a means of developing intellectual capital which will contribute to the country's economic growth. NIS is a network of laboratory schools for gifted and talented students with trilingual education where the best international research and education practices are implemented and tested and that are expected to be shared with the wider education system of education in Kazakhstan (see Yakavets, 2014).

References

Berman, K. M., Schultz, R. A., & Weber, C. L. (2012). A lack of awareness and emphasis in preservice teacher training: Preconceived beliefs about the gifted and talented. *Gifted Child Today, 35*(1), 18–26.

Bianco, M. (2005). The effects of disability labels on special education and general education teachers' referrals for gifted programs. *Learning Disability Quarterly, 28*(4), 285–293.

Bianco, M., & Leech, N. L. (2010). Twice-exceptional learners: Effects of teacher preparation and disability labels on gifted referrals. Teacher Education and Special Education. *The Journal of the Teacher Education Division of the Council for Exceptional Children, 33*(4), 319–334.

Bianco, M., Harris, B., Garrison-Wade, D., & Leech, N. (2011). Gifted girls: Gender bias in gifted referrals. *Roeper Review*, *33*, 170–181.

Borland, J. (1978). Teacher identification of the gifted: A new look. *Journal for the Education of the Gifted*, *2*, 22–32.

Brown, S. W., Renzulli, J. S., Gubbins, E. J., Siegle, D., Zhang, W., & Chen, C. H. (2005). Assumptions underlying the identification of gifted and talented students. *Gifted Child Quarterly*, *49*(1), 68–79.

Carman, C. A. (2011). Stereotypes of giftedness in current and future educators. *Journal for the Education of the Gifted*, *34*, 790–812.

Chan, D. W. (2000). Exploring identification procedures of gifted students by teacher ratings: Parent ratings and student self-reports in Hong Kong. *High Ability Studies*, *11*, 69–82.

Chan, D. W. (2008). Giftedness of Chinese Students in Hong Kong: Perspectives from different conceptions of intelligences. *Gifted Child Quarterly*, *52*(1), 40–54.

Elhoweris, H. (2008). Teacher judgment in identifying gifted/talented students. *Multicultural Education*, *15*, 35–38.

Elhoweris, H., Mutua, K., Alsheikh, N., & Holloway, P. (2005). Effect of children's ethnicity on teachers' referral and recommendation decisions in gifted and talented programs. *Remedial and Special Education*, *26*(1), 25–31.

Endepohls-Ulpe, M., & Ruf, H. (2005). Primary school teachers' criteria for the identification of gifted pupils. *High Ability Studies*, *16*, 219–228.

Gagné, F. (1994). Are teachers really poor talent detectors? Comments on Pegnato and Birch's (1959) study of the effectiveness and efficiency of various identification techniques. *Gifted Child Quarterly*, *38*, 124–126.

Gallagher, S., Smith, S. R., & Merrotsy, P. (2011). Teachers' perceptions of the socio-emotional development of intellectually gifted primary aged students and their attitudes towards ability grouping and acceleration. *Gifted and Talented International*, *26*(1–2), 11–24.

García-Cepero, M. C., & McCoach, D. B. (2009). Educators' implicit theories of intelligence and beliefs about the identification of gifted students. *Universitas Psychologica*, *8*(2), 295–310.

Grigorenko, E. L. (2000). Russian gifted education in technical disciplines: Tradition and transformation. In K. A. Heller, F. J. Mönks, R. Subotnik, & R. J. Sternberg (Eds.), *International handbook of giftedness and talent* (pp. 735–742). Oxford, UK: Elsevier.

Hernández-Torrano, D., & Tursunbayeva, X. (2016). Are teachers biased when nominating students for gifted programs? Evidence from Kazakhstan. *High Ability Studies*, *27*(2), 165–176.

Hoogeveen, L., Van Hell, J. G., & Verhoeven, L. (2005). Teacher attitudes toward academic acceleration and accelerated students in the Netherlands. *Journal for the Education of the Gifted*, *29*(1), 30–59.

Howley, A., Rhodes, M., & Beall, J. (2009). Challenges facing rural schools: Implications for gifted students. *Journal for the Education of the Gifted, 32*(4), 515–536.

Hunsaker, S. L. (1994). Creativity as a characteristic of giftedness: Teachers see it, then they don't. *Roeper Review, 17*, 11–15.

Jeltova, I., & Grigorenko, E. L. (2005). Systemic approaches to giftedness. In R. J. Sternberg & J. E. Davidson (Eds.), *Conceptions of giftedness* (pp. 171–186). Cambridge, UK: Cambridge University Press.

Kaiser, H. F. (1974). An index of factorial simplicity. *Psychometrika, 39*(1), 31–36.

Kim, K. H., Shim, J. Y., & Hull, M. (2009). Korean concepts of giftedness and the self-perceived characteristics of students selected for gifted programs. *Psychology of Aesthetics, Creativity, and the Arts, 3*, 104–111.

Lawrence, B. K. (2009). Rural gifted education: A comprehensive literature review. *Journal for the Education of the Gifted, 32*(4), 461–494.

Lee, L. (2002). Young gifted girls and boys: Perspectives through the lens of gender. *Contemporary Issues in Early Childhood, 3*, 383–399.

Lee, S. Y., Cramond, B., & Lee, J. (2004). Korean teachers' attitudes toward academic brilliance. *Gifted Child Quarterly, 48*(1), 42–53.

Matsumura, N. (2007). Giftedness in the culture of Japan. In S. Phillipson & M. McCann (Eds.), *Conceptions of giftedness: Sociocultural perspectives* (pp. 349–376). Mahwah, NJ: Lawrence Erlbaum.

McBee, M. T. (2006). A descriptive analysis of referral sources for gifted identification screening by race and socioeconomic status. *Journal of Secondary Gifted Education, 17*, 103–111.

McCoach, D. B., & Siegle, D. (2007). What predicts teachers' attitudes toward the gifted? *Gifted Child Quarterly, 51*(3), 246–254.

Megay-Nespoli, K. (2001). Beliefs and attitudes of novice teachers regarding instruction of academically talented learners. *Roeper Review, 23*, 178–182.

Missett, T. C., Brunner, M. M., Callahan, C. M., Moon, T. R., & Price Azano, A. (2014). Exploring teacher beliefs and use of acceleration, ability grouping, and formative assessment. *Journal for the Education of the Gifted, 37*, 245–268.

Moon, R. R., & Brighton, C. M. (2008). Primary teachers' conceptions of giftedness. *Journal for the Education of the Gifted, 31*, 447–480.

Niu, W., & Brass, J. (2011). Intelligence in worldwide perspective. In R. J. Sternberg & S. B. Kaufman (Eds.), *The Cambridge handbook of intelligence* (pp. 623–646). New York, NY: Cambridge University Press.

OECD (2014). Reviews of national policies for education: Secondary education in Kazakhstan. OECD Publishing. Retrieved from http://dx.doi.org/10.1787/9789264205208-en.

Pallant, J. (2010). *SPSS survival manual* (4th edition). London, UK: McGraw-Hill Education.

Pfeiffer, S. I. (2012). Current perspectives on the identification and assessment of gifted students. *Journal of Psychoeducational Assessment*, *30*(1), 3–9.

Phillipson, S. N. (2007). Towards of an understanding of a Malay conception of giftedness. In S. N. Phillipson & M. T. McCann (Eds.), *Conceptions of giftedness: Sociocultural perspectives* (pp. 253–282). Mahwah, NJ: Lawrence Erlbaum.

Phillipson, S. N., & McCann, M. T. (2007). *Conceptions of giftedness: Sociocultural perspectives*. Mahwah, NJ: Lawrence Erlbaum.

Pierce, R. L., Adams, C. M., Speirs Neumeister, K. L., Cassady, J. C., Dixon, F. A., & Cross, T. L. (2007). Development of an identification procedure for a large urban school corporation: Identifying culturally diverse and academically gifted elementary students. *Roeper Review*, *29*, 113–118.

Rouse, M., Yakavets, N., & Kulakhmetova, A. (2014). Towards inclusive education: Swimming against the tide of educational reform. In D. Bridges (Ed.), *Education reform and internationalisation: The case of school reform in Kazakhstan* (pp. 196–216). Cambridge, UK: Cambridge University Press.

Schroth, S. T., & Helfer, J. A. (2008). Identifying gifted students: Educator beliefs regarding various policies, processes, and procedures. *Journal for the Education of the Gifted*, *32*(2), 155–179.

Schroth, S. T., & Helfer, J. A. (2009). Practitioners' conceptions of academic talent and giftedness: Essential factors in deciding classroom and school composition. *Journal of Advanced Academics*, *20*(3), 384–403.

Sharma, J. (2012). Where are they? Gifted disadvantaged children in India. *Gifted Education International*, *28*(2), 215–223.

Shibata, A., & Forbes, D. (2009). Teachers' and counsellors' perspectives on gifted children and gifted education: New Zealand and Japan. *Gifted Education International*, *25*(2), 187–193.

Siegle, D., & Powell, T. (2004). Exploring teacher biases when nominating students for gifted programs. *Gifted Child Quarterly*, *48*, 21–29.

Siegle, D., Wilson, H. E., & Little, C. A. (2013). A sample of gifted and talented educators' attitudes about academic acceleration. *Journal of Advanced Academics*, *24*(1), 27–51.

Speirs Neumeister, K. L., Adams, C. M., Pierce, R. L., Cassady, J. C., & Dixon, F. A. (2007). Fourth-grade teachers' perceptions of giftedness: Implications for identifying and serving diverse gifted students. *Journal for the Education of the Gifted*, *30*, 479–499.

Sternberg, R. J. (2007). Cultural concepts of giftedness. *Roeper Review*, *29*(3), 160–165.

Tenenbaum, H. R., & Ruck, M. D. (2007). Are teachers' expectations different for racial minority than for European American students? A meta-analysis. *Journal of Educational Psychology, 99*, 253–273.

Ushakov, D. V. (2010). Olympics of the mind as a method to identify giftedness: Soviet and Russian experience. *Learning and Individual Differences, 20*(4), 337–344.

Yakavets, N. (2014). Reforming society through education for gifted children: The case of Kazakhstan. *Research Papers in Education, 29*, 513–533.

Chapter 8

Implementing Schoolwide Enrichment Model for talent development

Perspectives from students and teachers in Italy

Michael Cascianelli

Introduction

The extensive scholarly work of Renzulli and Reis (2014) in the realm of talent development and the implementation of the Schoolwide Enrichment Model (SEM) is a point of reference for school administrators, teachers and parents worldwide. The focus on independent learning connected to the inclusive context of SEM is considered a starting point for those schools fostering support for gifted and talented students. However, the fast routines of schools and the daily and constant changing needs of students do not always allow school administrators and teachers to question each of the steps for implementing a SEM based on Renzulli's scholarly work.

- Which are then the practical steps to start thinking of implementing support for gifted and talented students through a SEM?
- What issues are faced in contexts where there is no prior understanding or conceptualizations of gifted education?
- How do students and teachers perceive the implementation of such programmes?

Although the analysis of gifted education in Italy is not the focus of this chapter, it is fundamental to underline that there is no formalized scheme or structure provided by the Italian Ministry of Education regarding support for gifted and talented students. Over the last ten years, however, state and private schools have been implementing identification strategies of gifted and talented students. This first step is often originated by families of gifted students who face social or academic challenges at school and therefore need help. Moreover, teachers in Italy are now starting to be more aware that differentiation is also needed for those students who may be considered gifted and talented. As part of a PhD project at the University of Cambridge, a private school in Rome has started the first Italian investigation of a SEM based on Renzulli's work. The purpose of this study at Istituto Marymount, Rome was to design specific and individualized support for gifted and talented students through posing the following research questions:

- How do the teachers conceptualize giftedness within their school context?
- What are the pupils' experiences of being in class during the implementation of the enrichment programme?
- To what extent does the implementation of the enrichment programme bring about change at school?

This chapter will focus on the first practical steps taken to explore the implementation of SEM as a research project from its first beginning as a case study within five classes between February and April 2017.

Case study sample

The research project presented in this chapter was based at Istituto Marymount school where I worked as a teacher-researcher teaching music in Grades 4 and 5. Since September 2016, I had also been given the responsibility to design and coordinate a Schoolwide Enrichment Model Programme within the school. Istituto Marymount is a private catholic school in Italy and follows a curriculum approved by the Italian Ministry of Education.

The school is part of a school-network that comprises 19 primary and secondary schools which share the same values and commitment to education. This school is based in Rome and offers a bilingual curriculum in which 760 pupils study half of the subjects in English and half in Italian. Seventy teachers led by a primary school principal, a middle school principal and a headmaster work within the bilingual curriculum which also includes the study of Mandarin from Grade 1, as well as Latin and Spanish from Grade 6.

In an attempt to address my research questions, the research sample includes pupils, teachers and the leadership team of the school as well as parents. The pupils involved vary in age, gender, religion and ethnicity; however, they are divided into classrooms based on age groups as in regular schooling. For example, pupils attending Grade 1 of their studies will be either 5 or 6 years old, and pupils attending Grade 6 will be either 11 or 12 years old. Moreover, because the research is conducted in a private, fee-paying school, all pupils come from an affluent background. The latter consideration will need to be acknowledged in relation to the generalizability of research outcomes. With regard to the teaching community of the school, class teachers as well as specialists, such as music, art and gym teachers, were involved in iteratively questioning and developing their practices within the research project. The involvement of all teachers in the school, including specialists, was an attempt to improve the partnership factor within the research methodology.

After having presented resources on SEM to all the teachers of the school, I started to collect informal feedback from teachers to understand who would be particularly interested and motivated to take part in a study together with his or her class. In order to make this decision, I also had to consider my own teaching schedule that allowed me to have only a certain set number of hours a week to collect data in those classes. Furthermore, having three sets of classes for each grade meant that I also had to consider which classes to choose for each year group. Thus, the selection of classes was based on the following three criteria:

- Amount of time available to gather data
- Time slots available determining choice of classes
- Interest and motivation of teachers to implementing SEM

By following the above three criteria together with the head-master of the school, I decided to pilot the implementation with five classes between 3rd and 7th grades in order to have an illustrative set of classes that would provide the study with a picture of the experiences of teachers and students. This would also allow me as a teacher-researcher within the school to observe classes and interview teachers and students without disrupting my teaching commitments.

The school's teachers' population varies in age, teaching experience and nationality. However, all "classroom teachers" are female. Notably, it is important to underline that within the school's context the term "classroom teacher" is defined as those teachers who have responsibility for teaching different subjects only to a specific class and to keep a record of absences, students' overall performance across all subjects and well-being. This differs from the responsibilities of the so-called "specialist teachers" who are those who teach only a specific subject and need to report back to the classroom teacher. This refers to the music teacher, for example, who has responsibility for teaching the music curriculum to more than one class but does not have the above-mentioned responsibilities of the classroom teacher. The five teachers involved in the study are all classroom teachers who have been teaching in this school for the last two to eight years and they expressed interest in being part of the pilot study. Their interest was for a variety of reasons, such as promoting school improvement, using the study for a personal development, learning more about their class or learning more about gifted education.

In order to implement design experiments based on Renzulli's theoretical framework, the five teachers had to make two lesson plans based on two considerations taken from the academic literature:

- Renzulli's three types of enrichment activity;
- Renzulli's three Es – Enjoyment, Engagement and Enthusiasm (Renzulli & Reis, 2014)

As Reis and Renzulli (2003, 2009) suggest, Type I enrichment involves stimulating new interests in gifted children through exploratory activities. Type II enrichment includes critical and creative thinking and learning-to-learn skills through group activities. Type III enrichment aims to develop higher-level research and creative abilities through small-group or individual analysis of real problems.

Data-gathering approach: design-based research experiments

With the intention of addressing the research questions by exploring how to build a schoolwide enrichment programme in a private catholic school in Italy, the research study was carried out with design experiments within the school where at the time I was working as a teacher-researcher. Design-based experiments would allow the researcher to design and explore the whole range of innovations, whilst iteratively relating these innovations in order to develop domain-specific theories. As the DBRC (2003) argues, design-based experiments go beyond the mere designing and testing of particular interventions in a learning environment. Rather, design experiments "embody specific theoretical claims about teaching and learning" (p. 6), and reflect the purpose of understanding the relationship between theory, design artefacts and practice.

Cobb et al. (2003) propose five cross-cutting features of design experiments. Firstly, the aim of design experimentation is to develop a class of theories related to both the process of learning and the measures used to support that learning. Therefore, in order to investigate the building of an enrichment programme, the processes of learning advanced by Cobb et al. could involve the evolution and exploration of learning relevant to social practices within the school context. On the other hand, the measures used to support that learning might include teaching practices or even the negotiation of domain-specific norms between researchers and teachers. Pragmatically, as Cobb et al. suggest in the case of a school restructuring its practices, the theoretical goal might be to develop an "interpretive framework that explicates the relations between teachers' instructional practices" (p. 10).

The second cross-cutting feature advanced by Cobb et al. is the highly interventionist nature of design-based experiments. The research design elaborated when preparing for an experiment draws on prior research and, specifically, on the empirical and theoretical outcomes of that research. This systematic process of organizing the forms of learning being researched provides the study with a "measure of control when related to purely naturalistic investigations" (p. 10).

Thirdly, when implementing design-based experiments, a study needs to consider both the *prospective* and *reflective* aspects of these experiments. With regard to the prospective aspect, designs are developed with a hypothesized learning process in view and the means to support it. Hence, enrichment programme design experiments will be developed starting with the hypotheses resulting from the literature review. In relation to the reflective aspect, however, it is important to emphasize that these experiments are "conjecture-driven tests" that often lead to more specific conjectures and multiple levels of analysis. (Cobb et al., 2003, p. 10). Therefore, I will start the research with an initial design considered as a first conjecture about the means of supporting the development of an enrichment programme. This, however, will lead to framing more conjectures based on the iterative implementations with different classes, teachers and pupils involved in the study.

The latter issue of framing and reframing conjectures grounded in multiple levels of analysis will lead on to the fourth cross-cutting feature of these experiments, namely the iterative research design that will generate new conjectures to be developed and subjected to interpretation. This, therefore, will involve several cycles of creation and revision of new conjectures. Finally, the intended result will be an explanatory scheme that will provide the focus of the new conjecture and inform the next cycle of enquiry.

Furthermore, the fifth characteristic of design-based research methodology is again related to its pragmatic roots. The theories developed in the course of the research will focus on its domain-specific learning processes and will be bounded within the design structure. However, the theoretical outcomes resulting from the design experiments need to have the potential to genuinely work in the context. Therefore, the crucial question that needs to be asked in exploring the implementation of an enrichment programme is whether theory really informs the design and, most importantly, how it does so.

Challenges of design-based research experiments: validity and reliability

The employment of a theory-driven design to create elaborated intervention, to be improved by an iterative empirical process that will contribute to a deeper understanding of the underlying theory, exposes the research to considerable challenges (DBRC, 2003). In order to pursue the commitment to design a scientifically sound research study, it is of paramount importance to raise questions about design-based research in relation to validity and reliability.

In an attempt to promote validity whilst designing new conjectures grounded in previously tested and analysed experiments,

154 Michael Cascianelli

I would regularly find myself, as a teacher and as a researcher, in the dual intellectual roles of advocate and critic. In order to address this, triangulation of multiple sources of data will be of paramount importance to question my tacitly held assumptions. Similarly, reliability of findings can be supported by triangulating multiple data sources; however, because of the iterative structure of design-based research, this will need to be sustained with "repetition of analyses across cycles ... and standardised instruments" (DBRC, 2003, p. 7).

Regarding the validity of findings, it is important to underline the importance of the role of partnerships and the longitudinal iteration typical of design-based research studies. Hoadley (2002) reports that the help of teachers and participants in his study led to a fundamental reframing of the theoretical conjectures employed in the research design. However, this poses the logistical challenge of how to develop and foster productive and collaborative partnerships with teachers and other participants in the research context. For example, the research context of Istituto Marymount, Rome comprises 80 teachers working throughout early years, primary school, middle school and high school. Because of the longitudinal nature of design-based studies, the success of framing and reframing new conjectures will also be based on the strong commitment of both the researcher and the teachers. These partnerships and shared commitments will help to avoid misinterpretations of data and improve the validity of the research.

Design-based research experiments have the potential to provide robust explanations and innovative learning practices generated on theoretical and empirical grounds. The challenges relating to reliability and validity require the research to follow a rigorous and iterative process, which needs, however, to be open to reframing itself.

Ethical considerations

All research has to consider ethical issues in the course of the research design, when carrying out the study and when writing up any report. These considerations aim to inform all the research decisions that have consequences that might be potentially beneficial or harmful to participants and the wider research community in which a study is carried out. BERA's ethical guidelines for educational research (2011) state that it is in the interest of the participants involved in a study to have the opportunity to review the data gathered in order to respond to its authenticity. However, this might not always be feasible because of the large quantity of data gathered and the people involved in the study. In an attempt to address the latter issue, Miles and Huberman (1994) consider the authenticity of findings to be related to the internal validity of a study. Internal validity refers to the extent to which a study investigates what it purports to investigate. To address internal validity whilst allowing research participants to respond to the authenticity of findings, there needs to be evidence of persuasive connections between the conclusions drawn from the outcomes of design experiments and the methodology and procedures used to collect and analyse data (Evans, 2013). Therefore, this implies that both evidence of outcomes and the methodology used in the research need to be shown to, and discussed with, the classes and teachers involved in the study at the end of each of the design experiments. This was to be done iteratively by presenting the purposes of the study to the participants as well as showing how one activity in the enrichment programme may evolve into something different based on the participants' experience of that activity.

Furthermore, in order to maintain an honest and transparent approach when seeking permission, I made sure to provide the students' parents with an informed consent form to be signed. Moreover, in relation to the "self" and subjectivity of the researcher, it is of paramount importance to consider my dual role of teacher-researcher working at Istituto Marymount. As analysed by Taber (2013), detailed investigation into the learning process needs in-depth case studies of individual learners. My case study does not focus on the experiences of a small number of students, but rather on the perspectives of a large number of students and teachers in the school where I work. On the one hand, my dual role of both teacher and researcher could be very informative because of the access to information and the possibility to experience the contextual field of my research by living it every day. On the other hand, the same duality could be threatening and demoralizing for the participants of the study. Moreover, this may lead to potential considerations of conflicts of interest due to my designing, implementing and investigating the impact of the enrichment programme for the benefit of the school. Cooper (1993) has argued that researchers should seek to acknowledge the demands that our intentions place on the participants of a study. Moje (2000) has suggested that researchers should aim to make "positive" change in the lives of the participants of their studies, where "positive" is judged and desired by the participants rather than by the researchers.

In dealing with such issues, a "cost-benefit" analysis should be undertaken, acknowledging the following considerations:

- What will the participants be asked to "give" to the study?
- What benefit will the participants "gain" from the study?
- Who should judge whether the participants will benefit or not?

Methods

Teachers' interviews

Interviews with teachers can provide the study with in-depth data on a specific topic, depending on the questions asked by the interviewer. However, it is important to consider that an interviewer might fall into agreement or disagreement with the interviewee, and thus lose their neutral position (Lincoln & Guba, 1985). Moreover, I had to acknowledge that since the participants were aware of my being the designer of the programme, this might have biased the interviewees' comments. In addition, as Lincoln and Guba state, whilst a semi-structured approach to interviews is useful when the interviewer is aware of what they do not know, a semi-structured approach is useful when the interviewer is not aware of what they do not know.

Group data collection

In order to be consistent with my exploratory approach to case study and to address the research questions by investigating the experiences of pupils whilst implementing an enrichment programme, I conducted group data collection with class pupils at the end of each of the design experiments. In group data collection as well as in focus groups, "discussion is encouraged, and the researcher might be more interested in any consensus positions that derive from the debates rather than individual

Schoolwide Enrichment programmes 157

viewpoints fed in" (Taber, 2013, p. 277). However, group data collection differs from focus groups in terms of the level of input that I, as a researcher, offered to the pupils.

Finally, in order to allow the participants to reflect on how they responded in previous group data collection sessions, I chose to adopt video-stimulated recall and reflection (VSRR) during the course of the group data collection sessions. Research has found that VSRR has been shown to enhance reflection, especially by defining the focus and context for enquiry (Powell, 2005; Rosaen et al., 2008). With this in mind, I showed the pupils some of their classroom activities to remind them of aspects of the programme.

Participant observation

According to Cohen et al. (2011), participant observation allows the researcher to observe the participants in their natural context, and their social settings and behaviours within these settings. This was especially important when implementing design-based experiments to evaluate discrepancies between interventions. This immersion in the context and, therefore, in the data that was collected facilitated the generation of "thick descriptions" of critical incidents occurring during experiments.

iPad group data collection video recording

In addition to my participant observations, video recordings were taken to develop a more rounded understanding of the impact of the design-based experiments on the classes. The school has a large number of iPads for use in the classroom that are helpful in gathering data. During the pilot study, I operated iPads and made sure to record each activity by using its camera pointing to the class. Simpson (2011) argues that video recordings can provide a more unfiltered observational record than observations conducted by a human being. However, it is also important to acknowledge a possible limitation to filming in class: students may change their behaviour because they are aware they are being recorded.

Research diary

To address my research questions by triangulating data gathered from multiple sources, I decided to keep a research diary. As

158 Michael Cascianelli

Wilson and Fox (2013) suggest, diaries are a useful method of documenting opinions and reflections which may be difficult to report using a different method. Notably, I made diary entries on the same day on which I observed classes and interviewed participants in order to have a fresh memory of events that occurred.

To be consistent with the exploratory nature of the case study, each piece of text in the research diary was categorized with open coding (Strauss & Corbin, 1990). This allowed the generation of themes through the constant comparative method with codes emerging in one week being compared with new codes generated in the following week (Glaser, 1965).

Findings

Research question 1

Teachers' conceptualizations – relationship with others

All five teachers suggested that the impact of social interaction was key to supporting the relationship between gifted students and their classmates. The findings that emerged from data analysis of teachers' interviews and questionnaires suggested the gifted students in their classes were particularly isolated from the rest of the pupils, even to the extent of exhibiting lack of confidence and patience. The Grade 4 teacher claimed that "some of them are reluctant to say their opinion openly". Moreover, the Grade 5 teacher suggested that two gifted pupils in her class showed "little patience to respect the pace of the lesson and their peers". It is important to underline the fact that these categories were based on both the SEM implementation experience of teachers and pupils as well as teachers' preconceptions and past experiences. This is consistent with the theoretical perspective of constructive alternativism (Kelly & Kelly, 1963) adopted in this study that suggests there is no finite end to the alternative constructions of meaning that we may use. Thus, the teachers' perspectives will also serve to inform future constructions with regard to conceptualizing giftedness in the main study.

Teachers' conceptualizations – gifted characteristics

A second theme was formed by considering all categories representing gifted characteristics as suggested by the teachers.

Firstly, the level of curiosity of gifted students was regarded as the "main" characteristic by all teachers who referred to this, for example: "marked and silent curiosity". This, revealed by the data analysis, was seen as the most significant characteristic above everything else. Furthermore, teachers suggested originality and creativity as gifted features, linking them to a higher level of sensitivity of these students. The Grade 6 teacher claimed that "they demonstrate originality, inventiveness and precision". The latter consideration was then connected by the same teacher with the performance of these students in the classroom. She suggested that they have "the ability to think acutely and make logical inferences ... advanced thinking abilities".

Research question 2

Pupils' experiences I – organization impacting on focus of learning, homework and assimilation of information

FOCUS OF LEARNING

Students reported that the way in which the two activities were organized by the teacher allowed them to deepen their knowledge in relation to the topic. For example, the teacher in Grade 6 focused on exposing students to the same theme, namely the "Crusades" through Type I and Type II activities. As far as the teacher was concerned, because of the pressure of the prescribed curriculum she would have just been able to go through the material to be learnt and tell the students to study the material at home for the following lesson. On the other hand, students claimed that "by working like this we learned things in more depth" and that "by doing this in such depth we could even become more interested in a particular topic". The students' perspectives highlight the need to focus on learning within the activities. This, as the teacher argued, underlines issues related to the pressure of the Ministry's prescribed curriculum.

HOMEWORK AND ASSIMILATION OF INFORMATION

Furthermore, it was suggested by the students that the theme of organization had a positive impact on homework and assimilation of new information. The students in Grades 6 and 7 reported that the organization of the activities helped them to remember things better and in a more specific manner. Thus students claimed that "by organizing the activity in this manner I didn't have to study too much at home for the test because I could remember everything we had done in class" and that "at home I didn't have to work too much because I could remember the work done in class".

In comparison, students in Grade 7 highlighted the fact that working in this manner was useful not only in relation to homework but also to remembering new information more easily. Hence, students claimed that "in this manner we can learn more things and surely, we will remember these things more easily".

Pupils' experiences 2: group work related to friendship, expressing opinions and help provided by students

FRIENDSHIP

The students highlighted the impact of using group work throughout Type II activities. During the group data collection sessions students suggested that both activities allowed them to work more with their friends or even to make new friends within their own classes. Students reported that they "felt so happy that I was together with my best friends and by working together our friendship has improved as well" and that "by working in this way you can end up in group with other people and speak to them". The literature related to Renzulli's SEM (2014) provides examples of how enjoyment is key to allowing students to perform better and to engage socially with their peers.

EXPRESSING OPINIONS AND HELP PROVIDED BY STUDENTS

It was also suggested by the pupils that group work was meaningful at the level of sharing opinions with others. With this in mind, one pupil in Grade 3, talking about a Type II activity, claimed that "I would like to speak more ... in particular to show that I know many things and in this way I can do so". Similarly, pupils in Grade 4 referred to the same node concerned with sharing opinions, developing it to become that of sharing knowledge. Thus, pupils suggested that "everyone had their ideas and together we were able to build knowledge".

This theme that deals with sharing opinions, ideas and knowledge was present throughout the classes chosen for the pilot. Furthermore, one pupil in Grade 7 suggested that usually school does not give time for the students to say what they think about a specific topic and that through these activities they "had more freedom to express themselves".

Finally, the nodes related to pupils expressing themselves also led to identifying group work in relation to the level of help that students were able to receive from, and give to, their peers. A student in Grade 3 claimed that "if you don't know something somebody in the group might know it and together we can discover more things".

Similarly, Grade 5 students referring to their Type II activity suggested that "it was better to work in this way because when we did not know something we could help each other".

Research question 3

Change at school 1 – group work leading to change: groups' formation, enjoyment and change in performance

In presenting the first theme that emerged from the data analysis, it is important to highlight the fact that at an initial meeting teachers asserted that they were dubious about using group work. This was for several reasons, for example the pressure of the school curriculum impacting on the teachers' lesson planning or the feeling that pupils would get distracted. The data gathered from the pupils revealed in a number of instances that group work was rarely used in the classroom. Pupils claimed, for example, that "it is rare to work in groups; usually we work individually but when we work together it is more enjoyable". With the purpose of monitoring the impact of the implementation of SEM in the five classrooms, the teachers and I took into consideration their starting perspective and tried to design lessons to promote group work whilst still allowing them to monitor behavioural management, time management and content to be covered. All Type II lessons were video recorded and the videos were used to show video snippets to the pupils in order to stimulate recall and reflection during group data collection sessions.

GROUPS' FORMATION

The recurrent themes arising from teachers' interviews and group data collection's sessions underlined the fact that change was connected to the depth of lesson planning. In particular, this was also linked to the rigour with which teachers organized student groups based on personality traits and academic and social skills. Indeed, the teacher in Grade 3 reported that she "had to think carefully about the children ... their personalities but also their academic performance".

Although the teachers and I had decided to monitor specific aspects of the lessons through organizing group work, the students were responsible for allocating themselves different roles within the group. From my class observations I noted that "students are in groups of four to six children ... everyone has a specific role decided within the group".

STUDENTS' ENJOYMENT

The findings related to organizing groups and allowing pupils to assign themselves roles led to categorizing other findings related to students' enjoyment and performance. With regard to the former, all teachers reported an increase of enjoyment during Type I and Type II activities. This is suggested in the interviews with the teachers where they claim that "enjoyment and curiosity have improved in all students, even in the weaker ones" and that "the students themselves confirmed that those students who are usually indolent, they gave their best during the activities".

The change connected to increased enjoyment is suggested here as being related to three aspects of learning at different stages of primary and secondary schooling. Whilst the teachers in Grades 3 and 4 noticed an improvement in enjoyment and related to students' curiosity and behaviour, the teachers in Grade 7 suggest there was a change in enjoyment of those pupils who did not usually participate in class activities.

STUDENTS' PERFORMANCE

Regarding the change in students' performance during the implementation of SEM activities, the teachers considered performance to be bivalent and divided into specific knowledge and general knowledge acquisition. This was suggested by the teachers in Grades 6 and 7 where the content of the lesson was more challenging than for the lower-grade classes. By dividing the students into groups and allowing the various groups to concentrate on different parts of the same topic, the teachers underlined that "they were really prepared in their specific part and in their working in groups; however, in relation to the general part I think they would still need the teacher to systematize everything". Accordingly, a teacher in Grade 7 suggested that "whilst the group work allowed them to develop specific competences, the students would still need to work on acquiring general knowledge".

The latter comments on group work suggest mixed opinions on the part of teachers. On the one hand, the teachers seem to be considering the findings especially in relation to an increase in enjoyment. On the other hand, the teachers in the higher grades were concerned that the focus on group work led students to concentrate too much on specific knowledge and to forget that general knowledge had still to be acquired.

Change at school 2 – evaluating impact of exposing students to multiple resources: literature and new classroom experiences

A second theme that emerged when asking teachers and students what had changed with the implementation is concerned with the evaluation of the adoption of multiple resources during Type II activities.

LITERATURE

All teachers planned their lessons in such a way as to expose students to a wider range of literature compared to what the students would normally find in their course book. By exposing students to a larger and specifically chosen amount of literature to cover a certain topic, the teachers aimed to promote aspects of critical thinking as well as to develop group discussion. Two teachers reported that "it was useful to let them work on different resources, although it was not easy to find simplified ones for the topic" and that "it improved the enthusiasm and curiosity of all students ... even the weaker ones".

Moreover, during the group data collection session students reported that similar findings linked to the wider range of literature had a big impact on their learning compared to their usual lessons. Students claimed that during the activities they "had to choose the relevant information that we needed and we had to choose more than one resource to complete the activity". Accordingly, students in Grade 6 reported that "we had to compare literature and see which information would be more appropriate to use" and that "we interpreted the literature, we had to understand what it really meant and we had to choose the most important things" or "we had to analyse the literature". These instances suggest a shift in how students may use resources during an activity when exposed to an element of choice. In order to review the literature that was provided for them, the students had to analyse it and critically engage with it. As the students mentioned, this allowed them to choose the information that was most suitable for completing their work.

The findings suggested by the students might also have been influenced by the teachers' work in choosing and organizing the literature used during the activity according to the needs of specific groups of students. The teacher in Grade 7 claimed that she "divided the literature based on the groups that would have worked with it ... thinking about the students".

The above comment suggests an element of teaching and learning that has been widely discussed in the academic literature. This element refers to differentiation both for teachers who need to deliver lessons and for students who have different needs.

Finally, the excitement at having seen the students engage with a wider range of literature in a critical manner led the teacher in Grade 6 to suggest possible ways to foster critical thinking. During the teacher's interview she reported that the students did indeed enjoy selecting pieces of literature. However, she also suggested that although they enjoyed choosing pieces of information to complete several tasks, the next step might be to expose them to scientific literature reviews. This, as the teacher suggested, would allow students to start thinking in a scientific way, rather than merely selecting information based on group decisions.

NEW CLASSROOM EXPERIENCES

Whilst the majority of the teachers decided to use videos and digital content in Type I, the Grade 4 teacher worked on exposing students to different resources by inviting a parent as a guest speaker during a Type I activity and presenting a wider range of literature for a Type II activity. The purpose of the lesson was to allow the students to learn how to write for a newspaper and how to create an article based on pieces of evidence. This was new to the pupils and to the teacher who had never thought of exploiting the profession of a parent as a resource for use in the classroom. From the group data collection sessions, the pupils in Grade 4 reported that "by inviting the mother of one of our classmates we learnt from her professional knowledge and not from a page on the Internet where we don't know who has typed it". As suggested by the pupils, having an invited speaker bring her expertise into the classroom changed the students' experience of a lesson on a topic that could also have been taught by just using a regular course book. The impact of having the parent teach the students how to write an article for a newspaper made it relevant for them. As far as the teacher was concerned, this new experience helped the pupils to be even more motivated during the subsequent Type II activity in groups. The students enjoyed working to create their class newspaper based on the teachings of the parent. The teacher claimed that the students "were fully aware of the expertise of the person who was talking ... and that allowed them to experience something that 'adults' do rather than something for children".

The teacher suggested that since they recognized the profession of the speaker, the students were more interested than usual. Also, experiencing a Type I activity involving something that was not usually covered in their school curriculum led the students to feel that this was something of more interest to them. A pupil in Grade 4 stated that "by having a professional newspaper writer explain to us how to do things, we can immediately apply it and you can do it in a practical way".

Conclusions

This case study conducted on five classes at Istituto Marymount, Rome between February and April 2017 aimed to refine and finalize the research design to best inform the steps to take in a larger longitudinal study. During the six weeks of data generation and collection, the time constraints of both the teachers and myself as a research practitioner did not allow enough space to further investigate the teachers' perceptions. On the one hand, the interviews conducted with the teachers helped to develop their conceptualizations of giftedness and to provide the pilot study with their perspectives on how the activities went. On the other hand, also including group data collection sessions with teachers would have allowed a deeper understanding of what the research team as a whole thought about the students' experiences. The grades included in the pilot study were only those chosen among Grades 3 to 7. In each grade at Istituto Marymount there are three classes. However, this study illustrates only one class in each of the above-mentioned grades with their respective classroom teachers. This limited number of classes and sections for the study was based on my teaching timetable and my school commitments as coordinator of gifted education within the school.

Whilst a number of quantitative data-based studies have been found in relation to conceptualizing giftedness, there is still a lack of qualitative data-based research concerning the constant development of these conceptualizations in school settings. By allowing teachers to develop their conceptualizations of giftedness within their school context, the study aimed to construct a conceptual framework in which teachers could relate their views to a seminal conceptualization within the field of gifted education (Olthouse, 2014).

By investigating the perspective of teachers and students during the implementation of SEM at Istituto Marymount, Rome, this study aims to contribute to the development of the conceptualization of giftedness as well as to fill the gap in the literature related to strategies to support gifted students. Specifically, the proposed work does not only aspire to make a conceptual academic contribution to knowledge but more importantly to have an immediate, positive impact on the everyday lives of all students and teachers at Istituto Marymount, Rome.

References

British Educational Research Association (2011). *Ethical guidelines for educational research*. Southwell, Nottinghamshire: British Educational Research Association.

Schoolwide Enrichment programmes 167

Cobb, P., Confrey, J., Di Sessa, A., Lehrer, R., & Schauble, L. (2003). Design experiments in educational research. *Educational Researcher* 32(1), 9–13.

Cohen, L., Manion, L., & Morrison, K. (2011). *Research methods in education* (7th ed.). London & New York: Routledge.

Cooper, P. W. (1993). Field relations and the problem of authenticity in researching participants' perceptions of teaching and learning in classrooms. *British Educational Research Journal* 19, 323–338.

The Design-Based Research Collective (DBRC) (2003). Design-based research: An emerging paradigm for educational inquiry. *Educational Researcher* 32(1), 5–8.

Evans, M. (2013). Reliability and validity in qualitative research by teacher researchers. In E. Wilson (ed.) *School-based research*. London: Sage Publications.

Glaser, B. G. (1965). The constant comparative method of qualitative analysis. *Social Problems* 12(4), 436–445.

Hoadley, C. P. (2002). Creating context: Design-based research in creating and understanding CSCL. In *Proceedings of the conference on computer support for collaborative learning: Foundations for a CSCL community*. International Society of the Learning Sciences. 453–462.

Kelly, G., & Kelly, G. A. (1963). *A theory of personality: The psychology of personal constructs* (No. 152). W. W. Norton & Company.

Lincoln, Y. S., & Guba, E. G. (1985). *Naturalistic inquiry*. Newbury Park, CA: Sage Publications.

Miles, M. B., & Huberman, A. M. (1994). *Qualitative data analysis* (2nd ed.). Thousand Oaks, CA: Sage Publications.

Moje, E. B. (2000). Changing our minds, changing our bodies: Power as embodied in research relations. *International Journal of Qualitative Studies in Education* 13, 25–42.

Olthouse, J. (2014). How do preservice teachers conceptualize giftedness? A metaphor analysis. *Roeper Review* 36(2), 122–132.

Powell, E. (2005). Conceptualising and facilitating active learning: teachers' video-stimulated reflective dialogues. *Reflective Practice* 6(3), 407–418.

Reis, S. M., & Renzulli, J. S. (2003). Research related to the schoolwide enrichment triad model. *Gifted Education International* 18(1), 15–40.

Reis, S. M., & Renzulli, J. S. (2009). The school wide enrichment model: a focus on student strengths and interests. In J. Renzulli, E. J. Gubbins, K. McMillen, R. Eckert, & C. Little (eds.) *Systems and models for developing programs for the gifted and talented* (2nd ed., 323–352). Mansfield Center, CT: Creative Learning Press.

Renzulli, J. S., & Reis, S. M. (2014). *The Schoolwide Enrichment Model: A how-to guide for talent development*. Waco, TX: Prufrock Press Inc.

Rosaen, C. L., Lundeberg, M., Cooper, M., Fritzen, A., & Terpstra, M. (2008). Noticing noticing: How does investigation of video records change how teachers reflect on their experiences? *Journal of Teacher Education* 59(4), 347–360.

Simpson, P. (2011). 'So, as you can see ...': Some reflections on the utility of video methodologies in the study of embodied practices. *Area* 43(3), 343–352.

Strauss, A. L., & Corbin, J. (1990). *Basics of qualitative research.* Newbury Park, CA: Sage Publications.

Taber, K. S. (2013). *Classroom-based research and evidence-based practice: An introduction* (2nd ed.). London: Sage Publications.

Wilson, E., & Fox, A. (2013). Data collection. In E. Wilson (ed.) *School-based research.* London: Sage Publications.

Index

Note: Page numbers in *italic* relate to figures, those in **bold** to tables.

ability 3; above-average 72; acquired 4, 8; cognitive analytic 72; high 72; natural (innate) *see* natural ability
academic acceleration 80–82, 130; practical guidelines 82
Academic Olympiads 120, 140
accelerated learning 119
active listening 100
activities, out-of-school 122
addiction, Internet 48
adolescents: complex model for 53–55; gifted *see* gifted adolescents; negative expectations 52
alienation 44
anger 20–21
anxiousness 20
aptitude domains 5
assessments 82; of giftedness 23, 29–33; multidomain measurements in 31; of profile types 23; psychodiagnostic 92
asynchronicity (asynchrony) 13–14, 16, 34
asynchronous development 44, 50, 62
attention, practical suggestions 67
attentional disorder 34
autonomous learning model 79

awareness 44
awe, in students 113–114

Bartlett's test 133
behavior: compromising executive functions 65; delinquent 43; maladaptive *see* maladaptive behaviour; negative 55–56; types of 29
behavioral problems 13, 16, 47
bibliotherapy 101
boredom 77, 123; acceptance of 99
brain structure, and giftedness 61
bullying 49, 76–77

case studies: Giovanni 16–17; Istituto Marymount School, Italy 149–166; Kazakhstan teachers' conceptions 132–142
Cattell–Horn–Carroll (CHC) theory 32, 36n1
Central Asia 128, 131
central nervous system (CNS) 9
challenges 77–78; appropriate 97, 110, 121
children: characteristics of 12; difficulties encountered by 92–93; executive functions of 62; exploration of interests by 99–100; gifted *see* gifted children; identification of

170 Index

giftedness in 16–18; and learning challenges 62–63; support for 17–18; vulnerabilities of 13
classrooms, new experiences in 165
cluster grouping 83–84
cognitive analytic abilities 72
collaboration 82
communication, between school and family 95–96
componential intelligence 10
conceptions of giftedness study, Kazakhstan: conclusions 142–143; data analysis 134; discussion 138–141; limitations and future research 142; methods 132–133; participants 133; procedures 134; results 134–138
conflict 93
consistency, search for 13
coping 21
cortex 61; thickness and intelligence 64
cost-benefit analysis 156
counseling 21
creative domain 5
creative expression, opportunities for 98
creativity 10, 19, 159; measurement of 32–33
criticism 21
culture 5
curiosity 158–159
curriculum: appropriate 29; development 79, 106–107
curriculum compacting 79–80
cutoff scores 30–32

Dabrowski, K. 15
daily challenges 77–78
data collection 156–157
delinquent behavior 43
depression 14, 21
design-based research experiments 151–153; challenges of 153–154; ethical considerations 154–156
development, asynchronous 13, 16, 44

Developmental Model of Natural Abilities (DMNA) 7
differentiated instruction 72–73
Differentiated Model of Giftedness and Talent (DMGT) 5–7
discoveries 116–118
discrepancy 14
discrimination, and identification 139
dissincronia 14
downtime, and stress 17
dually exceptional students 33
dyssynchrony 14

ecological model (Bronfenbrenner) 53
education: of gifted pupils 72–73; provision of 136–137
educational fit 12
elitism 140
emotional factors 54
emotional handicap 21
emotional outcomes 76
emotional overexcitability 15
enjoyment 162
enrichment, activity types 73, 151
Enrichment Cluster (OWLETS) 74
enrichment clusters 83–84
enrichment programs 73–77, 120
Enrichment Triad Model 73
environment: forces in 4; interaction with 13; optimal living 93; stimulating 94; supportive 51
ethics 154–156
evaluation, of potential and risks 35
exam pressures 98
exclusion 14
executive functions 61; developmental 66–67; in gifted learners 64; practical suggestions 67–70; role at school 62–65; and skills 62–63; strategies for learning 70
exosystem 53, 55
Expanded Model of Talent Development (EMTD) 7
expectations, realistic 98

Index 171

extracurricular activities/programs
120; for gifted children 35
extroversion 55

failure 99; as feedback 97
family: communication with
teachers by 95–96; instability 93;
role of relationships 85; and
school 95–96; support 51; wider
members of 94
flexible thinking, practical
suggestions 69
focus: of learning 159;
maintenance of 66
free time 123
frequency, of re-testing
31–32
friendship 160
frustration 15, 19–21, 47;
tolerance of 68

Gagné, F. 5–7
gender: differences 55; stereotypes
46
genetic heritability 3–4
genius, notion of 10
gifted adolescents 43–46
gifted characteristics 158–159
gifted children 9, 35, 107
gifted education 72–73; Italian
study 148–149; purpose of
135–136
gifted learners, executive functions
in **64**
gifted programs 73–77; and
well-being 77
Gifted Rating Scales
(GRS)–School Form 30
gifted students 9; awe and wonder
in 113–114; challenging of
77–78; demographics of 141;
education of 72–73, 136–137;
identification of 129–130, 135,
143n1; independent work by
78–80; interventions for 80–82;
managing stress in 96–98;
observational skills of 112;
relationships with others 158;
in science 110–112

giftedness 6, 72; in adolescence
43–46, 53–55; American historic
definition of 10; in Asia 128,
131; assessment of 23, 29–33;
biological underpinnings of 7;
and brain structure 61; complex
model of 53–55; concept of
9–16; contextual 105–106; as
continuum 107; cultural aspects
5, 11; definition of 3–8; Gagné's
theory of 10; gender differences
44–45; identification of 23,
29–33; Kazakhstan study of
132–142; manifestation of 8,
134–135; multidimensionality of
32; Munich model of 30; nature
of 134–135; profiles of 18–23; in
science 105–108; as socially
constructed concept 128, 131;
teachers' conceptions of
129–132; tripartite model of 11;
types of 12, 18–23
gifts 7–8; genotypic foundations
of 7
goals: practical suggestions for
setting 68; unrealistic 15
grade skipping 81
grade-based acceleration 81
group work 161–163
groups 43; formation of 162

helplessness 21
hemispheric connectivity 61
high ability 72; in science 105–108
high potential, recognition of 34
Hikikomori 47–48
homework 159–160

identification: and discrimination
139; of gifted students 129–130,
135; of giftedness 23, 29–33; of
profile types 23
identity, development 47
imagination 123; laboratory of
116–118
imaginative overexcitability 15
implementation: barriers 82; of
SEM case study *see* SEM
case study

172 Index

impulse control, practical
  suggestions 67
inclusivity 140
individualization 121
information: assimilation of
  159–160; sharing 35
informed consent 155
inhibition, practical
  suggestions 67–68
initiation, practical
  suggestions 68
innate predisposition 8; *see also*
  natural ability
inquiring minds 114–115
insecurity 20
intellectual ability 11
intellectual domain 5
intellectual overexcitability 15
intellectualization 21
intelligence 3, 16–17
Intelligence Quotient (IQ) 10, 16,
  31; and academic success 62;
  and science 108
intensity 15, 34, 44
interests: exploration of 99–100;
  independent work on 78–80
Internet dependency 48
interpersonal growth 93
interruption, right time
  for 100
introspection 15
introversion 47, 55
intuition 44
Iowa Acceleration Scale 81
iPad group data collection 157
isolation 21, 55
Istituto Marymount School, Italy:
  gifted education in 148–149;
  SEM case study 149–166

Kaiser-Meter-Olkin (KMO)
  test 133
Kazakhstan 128, 131–132, 143n1;
  study of giftedness in 132–142
knowledge, systematic acquisition
  of 111–112

labeling 139
leadership capacity 22

learning: accelerated 119;
  disabilities 21, 33;
  individualization in 121;
  process of 97; too easy 62–63
listening, active 100
literature 163–164
loneliness 44, 47

macrosystem 53, 55
maladaptive behavior 33;
  management of 94–95
mental disturbance 33
mental factors 54
mesosystem 53
micro-teaching 122
microsystem 53; examples of
  54–55
misdiagnosis 34
monitoring, practical
  suggestions 69
motivation 47, 113, 123
motor skills 13
multi-potentiality 17
multiple intelligences 10
multiple resources 163–165
Munich model of giftedness 30
myths, about gifted children 9

natural ability 4–6, 8
Nazarbayev Intellectual Schools
  (NIS) 143n1
negative behaviors 55–56
negative expectations 52
new experiences, in classrooms 165
Noble, K. 12

observation 118–119
observational skills 112
'Olympiad'-type competitions
  120, 140
opinions, expression of 160–161
organization, practical suggestions
  68–69
organized disorder 100–101
original ways of learning through
  enrichment technology and
  socialization (OWLETS) 74
out-of-school activities 122
overexcitability 15

Index 173

parenting, styles of 52
parents: communication with similar others 95; context of 92; of gifted children 17; implications for 122–124; impotence of 50; practical suggestions for 34–35, 98–100; psychological support for 93–94; role of 46, 91–95; strategies for 19–22, 84–85, 100–101
parent–child relationships 50, 91
participant observation 157
peer recognition 76
peer tuition 122
peers: difficulty in finding 13; exclusion by 15
perfectionism 13, 15, 45, 47, 51, 96
performance 162–163
persistence, practical suggestions 68
personal characteristics 12–13
personal development 139
personal space 100
personality 18; disorder 34
Pfeiffer, S. I. 11
physical factors 53
placement 139
planning, practical suggestions 68–69
positive connotation 55–56
potential: evaluation of 35; realization of 45
practical suggestions 16–18, 55–56; on EF skills 67–70; for parents 34–35, 98–100
precociousness 34
prioritizing, practical suggestions 68
profile types: assessment of 23; identification of 23
profiles: of the gifted and talented 18–23; type 1: the successful 18–19; type 2: the challenging 19–20; type 3: the underground 20; type 4: the dropouts 20–21; type 5: the double labeled 21–22; type 6: the autonomous

learners 22; types and characteristics 24–28
programs: enrichment 120; pull-out 78
psychological distress 77
psychological diversity 47
psychological factors 53
psychological support paths 93–94
psychological well-being 12
psychomotor overexcitability 15
psychotherapists 33
pull-out programs 78
pupils, experiences of 159–161

questioning 114–115

rating scales, for teachers 30
re-evaluation 31–32
recognition, of high potential 34
rejection 20–21
relationships, with others 158
reliability 153–154
Renzulli, J. S. 73–75, 151
Renzulli Learning System (RLS) 84, 151
research diaries 157–158
research experiments, design-based 151–154
resource development 122
right time, for interruption 100
risk: evaluation of 35; factors 46–52; situations 54
Robinson, N. 12
rules, emphasis on 13

scholastic disaffection 92–93
school: change at 161–165; effect of type of 137–138; executive functions at 62–65; and family 95–96; role of 85
school administrators, pragmatic strategies for 84–85
Schoolwide Enrichment Model (SEM) 73–75, 79, 83, 148; case study see SEM case study
science: aspects of 108, 124; giftedness and high ability in 105–108

174 Index

scientific interests, of students 111–112
scientists: defining giftedness in 108–110; examples of great 109; spotting gifted students 110–111
scores, use of one test 30–32
segregation 140
self-awareness 46
self-concept 16, 22, 46; negative 19
self-criticism 51
self-directed learning model 79
self-efficacy 48
self-esteem 47, 80, 97
self-harm/injury 48–50
self-knowledge 15
self-regulation 63; imposition of 66; practical suggestions 69
SEM case study: conclusions 165–166; data-gathering approach 151–153; ethical considerations 154–156; findings 158–165; group data collection 156–157; iPad group data collection 157; methods 156–158; participant observation 157; research diary 157–158; research question 1 149, 158–159; research question 2 149, 159–161; research question 3 149, 161–165; sample 149–151; teachers' interviews 156; validity and reliability 153–154
sensitivity 34
sensorial overexcitability 15
sensorimotor domain 5
shyness 47
siblings 94; relationship with 96
skills 17; and executive functions 62–63; observational 112; social 98–99; uneven development of 13
social adjustment 14
social networks 44
social skills, promotion of 98–99
social withdrawal (Hikikomori) 47–48
socioaffective domain 5
special programs 120

Standards for Educational and Psychological Measurement 31
strategies, for parents 19–22, 100–101
stress 21, 77; and downtime 17; management of 96–98; parental 94
struggles 99
students: adolescent 43–46, 53–55; awe and wonder in 113–114; characteristics of 130; complex model for 53–55; education of 72–73; enjoyment 162; experiences of 159–161; gifted *see* gifted students; group work by 161–163; help provided by 160–161; high-potential 45–46; multiple resources 163–165; observational skills 112; performance 162–163; scientific interests of 111–112; talented *see* talented students
subject-based acceleration 80–81
suicide 49–50
support: activation of 35; for gifted children 17–18; paths 93–94
systems model, factors in 53–54

talent 6–7; definition of 3–8; development 7–8, 10; Gagné's theory of 10; hiding of 20; profiles of 18–23
talent areas, independent work on 78–80
talented students: challenging of 77–78; education of 72–73; independent work by 78–80; managing stress in 96–98
task completion 66
teachers: classroom 151; communication with family 95–96; conceptualizations of giftedness by 129–132, 134–137, 158–159; effect of years of experience 137–138, 141; implications for 119–122; interviews of 156; pragmatic strategies for 84–85; professional development of 82; program

development role of 29–30; role of 46; in SEM case study 149–166; specialist 151; spotting of gifted students by 110–111; strategies for 19–22; traditional views of 141
teaching: EF skills 67; effect of years of experience 137–138
teenagers: experience of world 44; systems model for 53–54
testing truths 116
time management, practical suggestions 69
Total School Cluster Grouping (TSCG) 83
Total Talent (TT) portfolio 79, 84
transversal factors 54
tripartite model of giftedness 11

truth, testing of 116
twice exceptionality 33–34
Type III activities within SEM 79

underachievement 14, 19, 29, 47; and family discord 51–52; and task repetition 80

validity 153–154
video-stimulated recall and reflection (VSRR) 157
vulnerability 33

well-being, and gifted programs 77
wonder, in students 113–114
working memory, practical suggestions 69

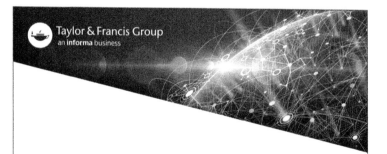

Taylor & Francis eBooks

www.taylorfrancis.com

A single destination for eBooks from Taylor & Francis with increased functionality and an improved user experience to meet the needs of our customers.

90,000+ eBooks of award-winning academic content in Humanities, Social Science, Science, Technology, Engineering, and Medical written by a global network of editors and authors.

TAYLOR & FRANCIS EBOOKS OFFERS:

- A streamlined experience for our library customers
- A single point of discovery for all of our eBook content
- Improved search and discovery of content at both book and chapter level

REQUEST A FREE TRIAL
support@taylorfrancis.com